KOSOVO: THE EVIDENCE

KOSOVO
the evidence

AMNESTY
INTERNATIONAL
UNITED KINGDOM

Kosovo: the evidence

Front cover photograph © Mark Seager: *Villagers dig up a grave to show
the burned remains of a village elder.
Doloro, May 1998.*
Inside photographs © Reuters . Photograph on page 22 © AP Photos

Printed by Ennisfield Print and Design
September 1998

ISBN 1873328311
AIUK Product Ref PB211

Contents

Kosovo province within the Balkans region.   Source: *The Economist*

Acronyms

AI Amnesty International
APC Armoured personnel carrier
CCP Federal Code of Criminal Procedure
CDHRF Council for the Defence of Human Rights and Freedoms
FRY Federal Republic of Yugoslavia
FYROM Former Yugoslav Republic of Macedonia
HLC Humanitarian Law Centre
HIWG Humanitarian Issues Working Group
ICCPR International Covenant on Civil and Political Rights
ICRC International Committee of the Red Cross
IFRC International Federation of Red Cross and Red Crescent Societies
IMF International Monetary Fund
KLA Kosovo Liberation Army
LDK Democratic League of Kosovo
NMLK National Movement for the Liberation of Kosovo
OHCHR Office of the United Nations High Commissioner for Human Rights
OSCE Organisation for Security and Co-operation in Europe
PHR Physicians for Human Rights
SDB State security police
SFRY Socialist Federal Republic of Yugoslavia
Tribunal International Criminal Tribunal for the former Yugoslavia
UÇK Ushtria Çlirimtare e Kosovës (Albanian name for KLA)
UN United Nations
UNHCR UN High Commissioner for Refugees

War crimes and crimes against humanity

War crimes and crimes against humanity have been committed in 1998 in the Kosovo province of Yugoslavia.

- Members of the Yugoslav army and the Serbian police have been responsible for enforced disappearances and the extrajudicial execution of civilian non-combatants. The Serbian police have engaged in the widespread torture of suspects, sometimes leading to their deaths. These acts constitute grave breaches of humanitarian law and international human rights law.
- Members of the Kosovo Liberation Army (KLA) have been responsible for the killings of people not involved in hostilities and for abductions and the taking of hostages. This is prohibited by Common Article 3 of the Geneva Conventions of 1949 and constitutes a serious breach of humanitarian law.

Although in a situation of much confusion and mass displacement, the exact death toll is virtually impossible to establish, several hundred ethnic Albanians and a smaller number of Serbs have been reported as killed since the conflict began in February 1998 between police and armed ethnic Albanians.

- Between 28 February and 6 March 1998 Serbian police killed at least 80 ethnic Albanians in the villages of Likošane, Ćirez and Donji Prekaz in the Drenica region of Kosovo. Although evidence was incomplete, it was clear that many of the victims – who included at least 12 women and 11 children – had no involvement in armed attacks.
- At least eight men, two of them over 60 years of age, were extrajudicially executed by Serbian police in the village of Ljubenic on 25 May 1998. Six days later, eight men from Novi Poklek near

Glogovac were 'disappeared' after being detained by police.

- At least 58 people, but possibly up to 200, were killed between 17-21 July in Orahovac, during and after fighting to capture the town. Some of these were reported to have been shot in extrajudicial executions. Some 20 Serbs and Montenegrins remain 'missing' following presumed abduction by the KLA, and 52 ethnic Albanians remain in Serbian police detention, where Amnesty International believes they are at risk of torture.

The 'disappeared'

The hidden victims of the conflict in Kosovo are those who have 'disappeared' following detention by government forces and those who are 'missing' following abduction by armed opposition groups.

- The International Committee of the Red Cross (ICRC) stated in August 1998 that it was investigating the cases of over 400 Albanians reportedly detained by Serbian forces. The United Nations High Commissioner for Refugees (UNHCR) gave a total of 400 gathered during its registration of those reported as unaccounted for. The UNHCR believes that around 200 of these are currently in police detention.
- The ICRC is also investigating the cases of 138 Serbs and Montenegrins reportedly abducted by the KLA. The Serbian Media Centre in Priština claimed that in the period between 1 January and 27 July 1998, the KLA had been responsible for the 'kidnap' of 171 people, 37 of whom had been released, seven had escaped, and 15 killed.

However, the confusion resulting from the massive displacement of families driven from their homes by attacks or fear of attack and unable to maintain contact with one another means that all figures for 'missing' or 'disappeared' people in Kosovo province need to be treated with caution.

The displaced

In August 1998 it was estimated that there are some 170,000 people from Kosovo province internally displaced within the borders of the Federal Republic of Yugoslavia. This is in addition to over 13,000 refugees who have fled to other countries such as Albania during the course of 1998. In the Tropoje district of Northern Albania alone there were estimated to be over 6,000 such refugees by August 1998.

A decade of torture and ill-treatment

For more than a decade, a systematic pattern of human rights violations against the majority ethnic Albanian population has occurred in Kosovo province – including torture and ill-treatment by police, deaths in police custody, and unfair trials for political prisoners. Lack of effective redress for these violations of basic human rights has contributed directly to the outbreak of the current conflict.

Key recommendations

1. Individuals responsible for planning or carrying out war crimes and crimes against humanity in Kosovo should be held to have personal criminal responsibility, in line with the principle established at the Nuremberg Tribunal after the Second World War. The international community should assist the International Criminal Tribunal for the former Yugoslavia in its efforts to investigate the situation in Kosovo province and to prosecute those responsible for war crimes. They should provide the Tribunal with all the necessary financial and other support required to carry out its mandate effectively.

2. The international community should provide financial resources and political support to an enlarged human rights monitoring programme of the Office of the United Nations High Commissioner for Human Rights (OHCHR) in the Federal Republic of Yugoslavia, enabling its field operation to monitor effectively human rights in the country as a whole, including an adequately staffed field office in Kosovo.

3. Given the fundamental human right to leave one's country and seek asylum, states should not pursue any policies that prevent those forced from their homes from obtaining effective protection across borders if necessary. States should respect the fundamental principle of *non-refoulement* of refugees, and share responsibility for those in need of international protection.

Of course, the primary responsibility for taking urgent action to improve the human rights situation in Kosovo province rests with the Yugoslavian Federal and Serbian National authorities.

Above and next page: An ethnic Albanian family, displaced from the area around Mališevo (July 1998)

Introduction
The road from Kosovo Polje

On 24 April 1987 a Serbian Communist Party leader travelled down from Belgrade to Kosovo Polje. He had come to hear the grievances of Kosovo Serbs, who were angry about perceived discrimination and frightened about their future in a province populated mainly by ethnic Albanians. As they met, a large crowd of Serbs gathered outside and scuffles broke out with the police, who started to use their batons. The man from Belgrade came out to address the crowd. As the television camera whirred, he said 'No one should dare to beat you!' and launched into a passionate speech about the importance of Kosovo for the Serbs. The crowd began to chant: 'Slobo, Slobo!'

Within two years, Slobodan Milošević had succeeded in taking over as president of the Serbian League of Communists and effectively abolishing the autonomy of Kosovo province[1] within Serbia by constitutional changes. The suspension of Kosovo's parliament followed a year later. Human rights violations by the Serb police against ethnic Albanians quickly formed a sickening pattern that has continued to this day.

Although the significance of that particular April day in Kosovo Polje, both for Milošević's own political career and for the subsequent history of the Balkans, has often been exaggerated, it helps to explain a dictum that can be heard everywhere in the former Yugoslavia: 'It all started with Kosovo, and it will all end with Kosovo'. The resurgence of Serbian nationalism and the implications of Kosovo's change of status for the federal politics of Yugoslavia were key steps to the

---

[1] Note on terminology: *Kosovo province* is the name that Amnesty International uses to describe the Autonomous Province of Kosovo and Metohija. *Kosovo* is how the Serbs spell the name of the province, and they pronounce it with a stress on the first syllable. The Albanians spell it *Kosova* or *Kosovë*, and pronounce it with a stress on the second syllable. Amnesty International uses the name *Kosovo province* to avoid taking sides or conferring recognition or legitimacy to either side.

disintegration of Yugoslavia in 1991.

Some commentators, of course, trace the road from Kosovo Polje a lot further back than 1987. Kosovo Polje, the 'field of blackbirds', was also the site of a famous battle in 1389 when the Serbian Prince Lazar fell to the invading Ottoman army, heralding over five centuries of Ottoman domination (although the site of the battlefield, to the north of Priština, is some way from the modern town of Kosovo Polje). Serb historians and politicians frequently refer to the battle of Kosovo Polje, as well as to the ancient monuments of the Serbian Orthodox Church which dot the province, when reiterating Kosovo's place at the centre of Serb nationhood. Ethnic Albanians, for their part, point to the other end of Kosovo, and the formation of the League of Prizren which in 1878 spearheaded the Albanian national revival.

The historical explanations and justifications which surround the current crisis in Kosovo province, however, often obscure the fact that different ethnic groups have co-existed in Kosovo for many centuries. When the Ottoman empire invaded in the 14th century, it in fact faced an army in which Serbs fought side by side with Albanians. As with mixed populations elsewhere in the Balkans, ethnic tension is more directly traceable to modern politics than ancient rivalries.

Another Bosnia?

If comment about the ethnic background to the conflict in Kosovo province is often misleading, so too are the frequent references to 'another Bosnia'. Enough has already been said to show that the situation in Kosovo province not only pre-dated the Bosnian conflict but also supplied the conditions that helped create it. In fact a decade of unaddressed human rights violations, as documented in this book, lies behind the current crisis in Kosovo province.

Two further important distinctions should be made between Kosovo province and Bosnia-Herzegovina, which have important implications for any potential resolution to the current conflict. Firstly, whereas Bosnia-Herzegovina was recognised as a separate state by the international community, becoming a member of the United Nations in May 1992, Kosovo is a province of Serbia in the Federal Republic of Yugoslavia.

Secondly, the demographic situation in Kosovo is radically different from that in Bosnia-Herzegovina. Ethnic Albanians now make up some 90 per cent of the population of Kosovo province, with Serbs forming less than 10 per cent. However, there are also sizeable ethnic

Albanian populations in the Former Yugoslav Republic of Macedonia, Montenegro, and the Sandžak region of Serbia, as well as elsewhere in the Balkans.

Amnesty International takes no position on the political status of Kosovo province, or its political relations with other states. But it can be noted that the political and demographic realities in the region have led to the international community combining verbal support for the democratic rights of Kosovar Albanians with a reluctance to countenance any form of independence or redrawing of state boundaries in Kosovo for fear of igniting a wider conflict in the Balkans.

Just as 'It all started with Kosovo' can be taken as referring to different events, so 'It will all end with Kosovo' can be interpreted in a number of ways. All too often in 1998, it seemed merely an expression of hopelessness.

Human rights and peace

Given the apparent intractability of the current situation, is there anything the international community can realistically do to end the conflict and widespread abuse of human rights in Kosovo province?

Since June 1998, various denunciations, threats and proposals have been made by inter-governmental organisations including NATO, the European Union, and the Contact Group on the former Yugoslavia which comprises the UK, France, Italy, Germany, the US and Russia. NATO military exercises have been staged in the region, intended as a warning to Slobodan Milošević and the Yugoslav forces.

Just as it takes no position on the political status of Kosovo, so too Amnesty International takes no position, whether in favour or against, on the issues of military intervention or economic sanctions. It is clear, however, that the various potential actions that have been discussed by the international community are primarily a response to the recent security situation in Kosovo province and fail to address the long-established pattern of human rights violations and the legacy of fear and resentment they have created. As such, they are doomed to prove inadequate.

If their basic human rights are in danger, communities can never feel secure. In an effort to protect themselves, or to safeguard their future, they are more likely to support armed conflict. Conversely, human rights guarantees are an integral part of confidence-building in any peace process. Understanding this link between human rights and

Policeman on an armoured personnel carrier, part of a Serb force securing an area in the village of Gornje Steoce near Peć after fighting with Kosovo Liberation Army members (June 1998)

peace – specifically a peace worth having – is central to a satisfactory resolution to the current conflict, and underlines why such a resolution will need to go beyond a diplomatic fix.

In mid-1998, the international media has shown the world the rapid deterioration of the security situation in Kosovo, and how even minimal respect for human rights is being withdrawn. The situation, however, was not new. This was a crisis waiting to happen. For more than a decade, Amnesty International has been warning of the growing human rights crisis in Kosovo province, where ethnic Albanians have been daily victims, particularly through the years when the world's attention was on the conflicts in Croatia and Bosnia. And just as the situation in Kosovo province is not new, so too it will not be resolved until lasting human rights guarantees are put in place that ensure protection for all ethnic groups.

Effective, independent human rights monitoring is essential in any situation where human rights have been gravely violated and risk being violated further on a massive scale, such as is the case in Kosovo today. Therefore, a properly constituted human rights monitoring mission must be at the centre of the international community's presence on the ground.

Scrutiny of Kosovo's human rights crisis is literally vital. Amnesty International's assessment, based on the presence of researchers in Kosovo province, is that only the high level of scrutiny given by the international media to the current situation has prevented the number of people displaced, 'missing', tortured or killed from escalating much further.

Crimes against the people of Kosovo

The people who suffer most from the outbreak of armed conflict in Kosovo province and the failure to address human rights violations are the civilian population. The primary responsibility for the war crimes and crimes against humanity that are taking place today in Kosovo does not lie with the Serb people. Nor does it lie with the ethnic Albanians. Both Serb and Albanian civilians have suffered from such crimes, and the responsibility for them rests primarily with their political and military leaders.

The distinction is an important one, for it points to a key role for the international community that has to date been overlooked. Recognising what is happening in Kosovo as crime, for which the responsible individuals should be prosecuted, is a key step in resolving the current human rights crisis.

'Bringing to justice those responsible for gross human rights violations could be vital to the re-establishment of lasting peace in a territory ravaged by war'

Richard Goldstone, former Chief Prosecutor of the International Criminal Tribunal for the former Yugoslavia

Prosecuting those responsible for war crimes and crimes against humanity does not just deliver justice to victims and their families: it also has a powerful deterrent effect. It sends a clear message that the international community will not tolerate these crimes, and that the full weight of the law will be brought to bear on the perpetrators. Those planning to commit such crimes will think again if they know they will be brought to justice.

The International Criminal Tribunal for the former Yugoslavia, based in the Hague in the Netherlands, has a jurisdiction which covers the entire geographical area of the former Yugoslavia, including Kosovo province. The Tribunal has a clear mandate to prosecute those responsible for war crimes and crimes against humanity in Kosovo.

Despite considerable financial and logistical difficulties, the Tribunal has proved more effective than is often given credit. By June 1998, 28 of the 78 individuals that had been indicted for crimes committed in Croatia and Bosnia-Herzegovina had been brought before the Tribunal in the Hague. However, some of the most important indictees, including Radovan Karadžić and General Ratko Mladić, have not been apprehended. The arrest of Karadžić and Mladić now could save lives in danger throughout the former Yugoslavia – including, most urgently, in Kosovo province.

The near-total lack of accountability for human rights violations in Kosovo province over the past decade has undoubtedly been one of the major causes of the current conflict. Justice has not come for the past victims; action is vital to prevent future victims. This can only be done by securing justice for the victims of today.

With every day that passes in 1998, greater numbers of civilians are falling victim to displacement, torture, and death in Kosovo province. The Geneva Conventions of 1949 and international human rights law are being blatantly ignored: war crimes are being committed in Kosovo today.

2

Kosovo province today

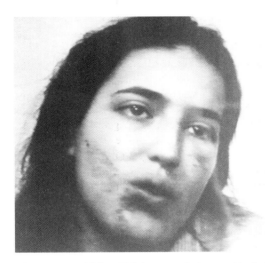

'Six policemen beat me yesterday, they hit me everywhere. They kicked me all over my body... they pushed me to the ground, pulled my hair. They turned me over to hit me on the back and then in the stomach.'

Nineteen-year-old Vlora Maliqi was struck down and badly beaten by Serbian police in Priština, capital of Kosovo province, on 18 March 1998. Her crime? To demonstrate against the recent killings of scores of ethnic Albanians in Kosovo province. Police beat or otherwise ill-treated ethnic Albanian demonstrators as they were leaving the demonstration. Vlora's friends managed to escape the police line. She was not so lucky.

How cheap is life in Kosovo province?

Kosovo province today is one of the bleakest, most fear-ridden places in the world. People unlucky enough to live there are suffering a human rights crisis. With every day that passes, greater numbers of Albanian and Serb civilians lose their homes. Many are tortured and killed.

The victims are mainly ethnic Albanians but include Serbs. They are subjected to a combination of deliberate and indiscriminate attacks by the Serbian police and the Yugoslav military. Many are killed or wounded, others suffer arbitrary arrests or abductions. Many have seen their homes deliberately destroyed. Albanian civilians in particular are coming under artillery, mortar and other weapons fire from the Yugoslav forces. Other ferocious attacks take place at the hands of the Kosovo Liberation Army (KLA), which also attacks civilians – Albanian as well as Serb. Excessive use of force seems to be the norm for both sides in the conflict. Local people who try to make contact with the Serbian police or KLA to assure them that they are unarmed and will not fight are still subjected to brutality. Civilians' homes are the targets of shooting or grenade attacks even before full armed conflict erupts in their localities.

Intensifying violence

Serious human rights violations have occured in Kosovo province for many years but these entered a new phase in February 1998. The 1998 armed conflict has given rise to rapidly escalating levels of violations, in particular forced displacement, extrajudicial executions and other unlawful killings.

Several hundred ethnic Albanians have been reported killed since the conflict began in February 1998 between police and armed ethnic Albanians, including the Kosovo Liberation Army (KLA), in the Kosovo province of Yugoslavia. The number of deaths grows each day, although in a situation of much confusion and mass displacement, the exact death toll is virtually impossible to establish. The police have killed, tortured and ill-treated ethnic Albanians in response to attacks upon them. A smaller number of Serbs, including police officers, were reported to have been killed by armed ethnic Albanians since the beginning of the year. Some 170,000 people, mostly ethnic Albanians, were reported to have been displaced from their homes.

Between 28 February and 6 March police killed at least 80 ethnic Albanians in the villages of Likošane, Ćirez and Donji Prekaz in the Drenica region of Kosovo. Although evidence was incomplete, it was clear that many of the victims – who included at least 12 women and 11 children – had no involvement in the attacks on police. Indeed, Amnesty International visited the country in March and collected testimonies describing police officers killing a number of the victims.

Police beat ethnic Albanian demonstrators, including women, who protested about the killings and the increasing police violence. In March one such demonstrator was shot dead in Peć and five others were wounded by police. Clashes with police and the Yugoslav Army continued with increasing frequency after these incidents and reports of possible unlawful killings escalated. There were also reports of the abduction and ill-treatment of Serbs by the KLA.

Although in many cases it appeared that the police policy was to shoot rather than take prisoners, police arrested dozens of men who were accused of 'terrorism'. Some men, who were reportedly abducted by police, remain 'missing'. In May, Amnesty International demanded justice and not 'trial by truncheon' as detainees faced convictions in unfair trials after being tortured during interrogation.

Bombardment and sniper attacks

One of the most extensive police and army actions began in late May 1998 around Decane in western Kosovo province. It produced many of the tens of thousands of refugees and displaced persons now in the region. The Yugoslav authorities evidently intended to clear the ethnic Albanian population out of the zone between the border and the central Drenica area. There appears to have been no attempt to locate military targets. Villages have come under bombardment, while sniping makes movement unsafe for civilians as well as KLA members. The police or army then move into villages one by one, often to find their inhabitants have already fled.

After their villages are attacked, many people who flee wait for hours or days in sight of their homes, before the spectacle of looting and houses burning forces them to give up hope of a speedy return. Even after escaping the conflict zone civilians feel far from safe. Men interviewed by Amnesty International in northern Montenegro, displaced from Kosovo, said they feared the presence of the Yugoslav army in Montenegro, and possibly also Serbian police there. A group of about half a dozen men told us that they were badly beaten by soldiers when they crossed into Montenegro.

Most victims are ethnic Albanians, but restricted access and the huge population displacement in the Decane area mean that much more time will be needed to document and verify the full extent of human rights violations. Within the displaced and refugee populations people struggle to make contact with family members from whom they are separated, and who may be among the missing or dead.

Among dozens of other ethnic Albanians unaccounted for from other parts of Kosovo are people who were seen being detained by the police. At the same time there are reports of abductions of Serbs by armed ethnic Albanians.

Police attack village

On 25 May 1998 a civilian car was shot at close to the village of Ljubenić. Three men in the car were hit: the driver, a police officer and an off-duty reserve police officer.

Terrified that their village would be attacked in retaliation, some of the ethnic Albanian men of Ljubenić reportedly tried to pass a message to the police that there were no arms or armed men in the village. There was no chance for any such message to be sent. Before long, a large police force, some in armoured vehicles, arrived at Ljubenić. They fired on the Albanian part of the village with artillery and other weapons for up to 30 minutes, before entering the village itself. According to witnesses, the 20 or so houses occupied by Serbs remained untouched.

By the time the police arrived, most villagers had fled to the nearby woods. Those who could not escape sheltered in their own or neighbours' houses as best they could. Police forced their way into a house where about 14 people was sheltering and ordered the occupants out. They beat the men, who were unarmed, then ordered them to run and shot them while they were running. Four men were killed in this incident. In another compound, a further eight men were killed in a similarly brutal fashion.

Most of the villagers who fled crossed the border into Albania to become refugees or into Montenegro to become internally displaced persons. They have little chance of returning in the immediate future: the police set houses on fire during the operation.

On 29 May police reportedly fired at Ljubenić again with mortar rounds and other weapons, causing the few villagers who had remained to flee. The village was left deserted.

The mass graves of Orahovac

Between 17 and 21 July 1998, in a town called Orahovac, almost all the dimensions of Kosovo's human rights tragedy were played out in one place. Reports and allegations of what happened in Orahovac are often conflicting, based on unverified published data or subject to deliberate disinformation promoted at times by both sides in the conflict and their supporters.

A picturesque town with a peacetime population of 200,000 – approximately 80 per cent Albanian, the remainder a mix of Turks, Slav Muslims, Roma, Montenegrins and Serbs – Orahovac is distinctive for its narrow cobblestone streets and closely-packed stone-roofed houses. Located 60 km southwest of Priština, Orahovac was the first attempt by the Kosovo Liberation Army to seize control of a major population centre. Serbian police and Yugoslav military reinforcements were brought in, the counter-attack beginning with sustained bombardment from mortars or light artillery fire. There were no outside observers to events at Orahovac as they unfolded from 17 July until journalists and humanitarian aid workers were allowed to enter the town on the afternoon of 21 July, after the fighting had subsided.

There were fresh grave sites in Orahovac and in the nearby city of Prizren which police claim hold a total of 51 bodies of those killed in fighting during the armed confrontation at Orahovac; all 51 are claimed by police to be the bodies of KLA combatants. The graves were dug and the bodies hastily interred on or around 21 July, without independent observers being present. There has been no suggestion that autopsies were carried out on them.

Escorting journalists to the Orahovac grave site where it was claimed 40 bodies were buried, a Serbian Interior Ministry spokesperson, Col. Božidar Filić, on 5 August stated that the total number of bodies found after the armed confrontation of 17-21 July was 58 (53 men and five women), five of which had been claimed by and handed over to families. Of the others, some have not been properly identified, and their burials have been recorded with a number only. This Orahovac grave site, not previously used for burials, is next to a rubbish dump on the eastern edge of town. On the night of 5-6 August one of the 11 bodies at the Prizren grave, located on the edge of an established Muslim cemetery, was disinterred and removed by unknown persons.

The reason for the escorted trip to the Orahovac grave on 6 August was apparently to seek to refute widely reported allegations made the day before of a more extensive mass grave, or multiple mass graves, containing the dead of Orahovac, and of casualty figures of over 500. None of these reports has been substantiated. European Union monitors who were urgently despatched to Orahovac on 5 August stated afterwards that there was 'no evidence of mass grave', albeit the grounds on which they made this conclusion have not been made clear: they did not reportedly conduct any excavations, for example.

The death toll certainly exceeds the 58 officially admitted burials, however. Ethnic Albanians in Orahovac have stated that they themselves buried dead relatives in private gardens and other plots. A figure frequently cited by ethnic Albanian sources during the first week of August, and said to be based on accounts by local people, is of around 200 dead. Local organisations have attempted to compile lists of the confirmed dead, and some of these – containing between two and four dozen names – have been published. On 7 August the organisation Physicians for Human Rights described as 'credible' reports of trucks containing corpses leaving Orahovac immediately after the end of the fighting, and called among other things for US aerial reconnaissance and US satellite

Scattered belongings and traces of blood in a street in Orahovac, scene of clashes between the Kosovo Liberation Army and Serbian forces (July 1998)

photography of 'possible grave sites' in and around Orahovac.

There exist numerous testimonies detailing possible extrajudicial executions at Orahovac, including the killing of 76-year old Sheh Muhedin Shehu – a well-known and venerated figure in the town – and those with him at his seminary.

The aftermath

Immediately after the fighting in Orahovac some 55 Serbs and Montenegrins, including an ambulance crew, were reported 'missing' from the town and the surrounding area. Thirty-five who had been in the custody of the KLA, among them seven Serbian Orthodox monks and a nun, were later released to representatives of the International Committee of the Red Cross (ICRC). On 6 August a group of 40 relatives of those still 'missing' held a demonstration in Priština calling for help in locating their family members, whom they believed were also in KLA hands, and in negotiating their release.

There were unsubstantiated reports that the KLA deliberately and arbitrarily killed some of those it had abducted in retribution for its expulsion from Orahovac.

One of those who still remains 'missing' from Orahovac is Djordje Djorić, a 28-year-old ethnic Serb, who on 17 July was driving a pregnant neighbour to the local medical centre and was stopped by a group of armed men who reportedly told him that they knew he had two brothers serving in the police force and questioned him. They then took him to the hospital, where he was detained overnight. In the morning he was further questioned about his brothers and reportedly beaten, after which he was driven away in his own car to an unknown destination.

According to Serbian Interior Ministry spokesperson Col. Filić, speaking on 5 August, 325 ethnic Albanian men had been taken in to help police with their inquiries in the aftermath of the fighting at Orahovac. For 52 of them, he claimed that it had been 'established beyond reasonable doubt that they took part in terrorist attacks', albeit up to that point they had not apparently been brought to trial. The others were released.

Local monitors, including the Council for the Defence of Human Rights and Freedoms in Priština, have published claims that many of those detained and later released have reported being tortured or ill-treated. As described elsewhere in this book, the torture and ill-treatment of ethnic Albanians in police custody is a well documented phenomenon extensive throughout Kosovo for many years.

With the onset of armed confrontation a large part of the population of

200,000 in Orahovac fled. Estimates varied, but the number of people who fled while the conflict was going on appears to have been in the range of 13,000 to 15,000. What happened to many of them next, as reported mainly by the humanitarian aid agencies operating in Kosovo province, is all too typical of the plight of the internally displaced in Kosovo.

The main flight route of the displaced from Orahovac was in the direction of Mališevo, around 15 km to the northeast. Conditions for the displaced in that town and nearby villages where they were accommodated – mostly in private homes – were described as problematic: humanitarian aid agencies reported that at Mališevo the displaced included many wounded, including women and children, but local health workers were reported to be unable to treat the seriously ill or injured because of a shortage of medicines and the ongoing suspension of the electricity and running water supplies to Mališevo.

On or shortly before 28 July the KLA decided to abandon Mališevo as Serbian police advanced on it. Most local civilians as well as those already displaced there from Orahovac were reported to have fled Mališevo in panic in the course of the previous four days into the small villages around Mališevo, and the nearby woods and hills. It was feared they were cut off from adequate food and water supplies, and were beyond the reach of humanitarian agencies which initially could not locate many of them. For example, the office of the United Nations High Commission for Refugees (UNHCR) reported that, after searching for two days for the estimated thousands of people displaced from Mališevo, its delegates on 30 July found a group of around 500 people in the woods around Crnovrata, west of Mališevo. They were described as 'in a desperate situation, huddled in families of up to 20 members, totally exposed, with only trees serving as their shelter. They had taken refuge in these woods for three or four days, without running water and with limited food supplies which they had brought with them when fleeing Mališevo.'

What happened in Orahovac in the terrible summer of 1998 is but one series of events in the human rights tragedy in Kosovo today. Every one of the people forced to flee their homes as a result of the violence in Kosovo province has their own terrifying story to tell. Their minds are seared with horrific images: walking along rows of dead bodies before they could identify those of their families; digging mass graves; their homes and villages burning behind them as they flee.

3

A divided people and a parallel state

The Federal Republic of Yugoslavia is made up of two republics: Montenegro and Serbia. These are the only two republics now remaining in what is still called Yugoslavia after the former Socialist Federal Republic of Yugoslavia disintegrated in 1991-92. For this reason, Yugoslavia now is sometimes referred to as Serbia and Montenegro or even just as Serbia. The Republic of Serbia includes two provinces, Vojvodina in the north and Kosovo in the south. Whereas 'Serbians' is the name given to citizens of Serbia, Serbs are an ethnic group. Serbs constitute a majority of the population in Serbia, but a minority in Kosovo province. Kosovo province (whose official title is the Autonomous Province of Kosovo and Metohija) borders onto the republic of Montenegro, onto Serbia itself, and onto Albania and the Former Yugoslav Republic of Macedonia.

The people

Nine-tenths of the population of Kosovo province are ethnic Albanians (predominantly Muslims, but with some Roman Catholics). The rest of the population are mostly Serbs (Christians of the Serbian Othodox Church), speaking a completely different language to the Albanians. There are also a small number of people from other ethnic groups in Kosovo province, including Roma and Muslim Slavs.

Kosovo, which has been inhabited for centuries by a mixed population, occupies a major place in the national consciousness of both the Serbs and the Albanians. It has become the focus of competing claims and ethnic conflict, which frequently involves appeals to history. For the Serbs, it is the heartland of the medieval Serbian kingdom where many of the greatest monuments of the Serbian Orthodox Church are located. The majority ethnic Albanian population recalls that it was in Kosovo that the Albanian national revival began, with the founding of the

League of Prizren in 1878.

After the second world war Yugoslavia saw major improvements in the status of ethnic Albanians in Yugoslavia. For the first time they were recognised as a distinct national group; the Albanian language was recognised as one of Yugoslavia's official languages and Albanians gained the right to education in their language. These gains were undermined, however, by the repressive policies enforced in Kosovo, for which Alexander Rankovic, a Serb, vice-president of Yugoslavia and chief of the state security police, has generally been held responsible. After the disgrace of Alexander Rankovic in 1966,

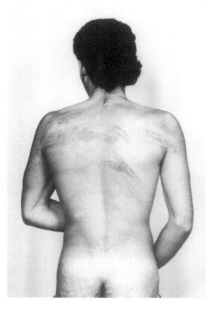

'On the 4 October 1991 at about 10.30am, in the centre of Peć, four police officers in a car stopped and asked to see my identity card and that of two friends with me. They took me off to the police station, beating me and swearing at me. They continued beating me with truncheons, and kicking and punching me, until my face was covered in blood. Then they beat my hands and back with truncheons (about 30 blows). Later they took me to another room where they continued beating me with truncheons on my hands, legs and back. They demanded to know where I had hidden weapons, and ballot papers for the referendum. Because I denied having these things, they beat me again, demanding that I collaborate with them. After a pause, they beat me yet again and cursed and swore at me. They made me take off my socks and wipe my blood from the floor. This went on until 3.30pm when they took me to court, with my face and clothes covered in blood. Since the court was crowded my turn came at 8pm. I was sentenced to 20 days' imprisonment... They also took a gold chain belonging to me.'

Daut Krasniqi, a secondary school pupil from Vranoc, Peć commune.

Serbs and Montenegrins lost their dominance in the political and administrative apparatus of Kosovo which became increasingly Albanian. This process was reinforced in 1974 when a new constitution gave Serbia's two provinces, Kosovo and Vojvodina, considerable autonomy.

At the same time Kosovo province experienced significant demographic changes characterised by the high growth rate of the Albanian population and the emigration of Serbs and Montenegrins (over 30,000 reportedly left the province in the decade from 1971 to 1981). However, in recent years Serb refugees from Croatia and Bosnia have been placed in Kosovo province, and measures introduced to prevent Serbs from selling land to ethnic Albanians. Attempts to attract Serb settlers to Kosovo province met with very limited success, despite government assurances of employment and accommodation.

Serb policeman in Junik, a village stronghold of the Kosovo Liberation Army seized by Serb forces after a three-week battle (August 1998)

Ethnic Albanian students in Pristina in October 1997. This peaceful demonstration was later violently broken up by Serb police

The relative growth of the Albanian population continued – until the current conflict at least. This was due to a number of inter-related factors, including the continuing high birth rate of ethnic Albanians, the relatively greater urbanisation of the Serb population, a notably high rate of abortions among Serbs, and the decline among Albanians of the traditional blood feud which had been responsible for the early deaths of significant numbers of adult males.

A battered economy

Though naturally rich in resources, including large deposits of lead, zinc, nickel and magnesium, Kosovo province is economically one of the poorest regions in the Balkans. It is the most heavily populated region in the Federal Republic of Yugoslavia and suffers from high unemployment. Following large-scale dismissals from state enterprises, most Albanians are dependent on small businesses or, often, money from relatives working abroad. People bringing foreign currency from abroad are often the target of police road checks, frequently leading to the confiscation of the money and ill-treatment. Such economic problems have exacerbated the growing nationalist unrest among ethnic Albanians.

Serbia itself is nearly bankrupt. About a quarter of its workforce is unemployed, and industrial output lower than before the war which racked the former Yugoslavia in the early 1990s. It has scant foreign exchange reserves. Slobodan Milošević, now Federal President, claims to want to reform the economy; members of his government believe Yugoslavia needs access to foreign credit to achieve reform. But sanctions deny Serbia membership of international financial institutions such as the World Bank and International Monetary Fund (IMF), making it impossible to benefit from foreign capital.

'Mr Milošević now faces an apparently straightforward choice: end Yugoslavia's isolation and undertake real reform, risky as that would be, or accept the certainty of continued economic decline. .... If he does not use this opportunity to surrender war criminals, push the Serb republic to honour Dayton and, above all, make Yugoslavia a country capable of commanding the allegiance of its minorities, the chances are that he never will.'

The Economist, January 1998

Ethnic division in Kosovo

When in July 1990 the Serbian parliament suspended Kosovo's parliament and government after Albanian deputies of the Kosovo parliament declared Kosovo independent, the economic and social infrastructure of the province began to divide on ethnic lines. Most ethnic Albanians working in the state sector lost their jobs, frequently dismissed because they had taken part in protests. Mass sackings of Albanian teachers occurred when they protested at changes introduced into the education system.

The majority of ethnic Albanians refused to recognise Serbia's authority in the province and started to establish 'parallel' institutions, including a parliament, a president, taxation and their own education and health systems. Ethnic Albanians largely supported the main ethnic Albanian political party, the Democratic League of Kosovo (LDK), which, while calling for Kosovo to be recognised as an independent state, has consistently advocated the use of peaceful means. The LDK worked to establish an entire 'parallel state' with the LDK leader, Ibrahim Rugova, as its president.

Parallel institutions are funded by a voluntary tax levied on ethnic Albanians in Kosovo province and the large number of Kosovo Albanians now living abroad. Although this revenue has sustained a social infrastructure, however, it is one whose hallmark is deprivation: the standards and facilities in the clinics are rudimentary; educational classes take place in private houses and produce qualifications that are next to valueless.

But perhaps the most disturbing division of all occurred in the police force. Ethnic Albanians claim that some 4,000 Albanian police officers were dismissed from their posts after 1990 after refusing to accept the measures introduced in Kosovo province by the Serbian government. As the confrontation continued, officers of the now largely Serb police force increasingly resorted to the routine use of violence.

Over the years as thousands of ethnic Albanians were beaten or otherwise ill-treated by police, and hundreds imprisoned after unfair trials, a dangerous legacy of bitterness accumulated among many ethnic Albanians. Their leaders warned, as did external commentators, that unless urgent steps were taken to resolve Kosovo's problems by peaceful negotiation, popular support might grow for those ethnic Albanians who advocated violence.

4

A decade of mounting violence

Ismet Krasniqi was among a group of parents of children at the Xhemail Kada primary school in Peć who went to the school on 29 January 1992 to protest to the school director about the Serbian curriculum. Together with several other parents, he was arrested by police, taken to a police station and beaten. He was accused of having organised a mass protest by parents.

On 30 January 1992 Ismet Krasniqi was examined by a doctor. He was found to have bruising to both buttocks, feet and hands. His left ear drum was perforated.

A systematic pattern of abuse

Ethnic Albanian unrest, exacerbated by economic problems, resurfaced dramatically in 1981 when there were widespread demonstrations in support of the demand that Kosovo cease to be part of Serbia and be granted the status of a republic. The demonstrations were halted in bloodshed. Amnesty International later learned that the Central Committee of the League of Communists was informed that over 300 people were killed, although published reports claimed no more than 11 dead.

A brief history of Kosovo province

1389
Serbian kingdom suffers defeat by the Turks at the Battle of Kosovo Polje, and becomes part of the Ottoman Empire.

1878
The League of Prizren is founded in Kosovo, marking the beginning of the Albanian national revival.

1912
Serbs bring Ottoman rule to an end in the 1912 Balkan War.

1918
Kosovo included in the newly-created Yugoslav kingdom

1941
After conquest by German and Italian troops, most of Kosovo administered by Albania under Italian control

1945
Kosovo reverts to Serbia within Yugoslavia, under Tito

1974
Under the Constitution of the Socialist Federal Republic of Yugoslavia Kosovo province is given considerable autonomy, including its own government and parliament, constitutional court, supreme court and representatives in all federal institutions. Kosovo already has its own university where ethnic Albanian students are taught in their own language.

1980
Tito dies

1981
State of emergency declared, following widespread demonstrations in Kosovo by Albanian nationalists, demanding that the province be given full republican status.

1987
The League of Communists of Serbia, under Slobodan Milošević, commits itself to reasserting Serbian control over Kosovo.

1989
Autonomy of Kosovo province effectively abolished by constitutional changes.

1990
Kosovo parliament and government suspended by the Serbian parliament after ethnic Albanian deputies of the Kosovo parliament declared Kosovo independent of the Republic of Serbia. Kosovo's ethnic Albanians start to establish parallel institutions, including a parliament, a president, taxation and their own education system. Majority of ethnic Albanians support Democratic League of Kosovo, led by Ibrahim Rugova.

1995
Dayton peace deal agreed — not covering Kosovo province.

1996
Milošević and Rugova sign agreement to get Albanian students back into state education buildings.

1996 on
Attacks on Serbian police and Serbs or Albanians associated with the authorities increase; responsibility for many attacks claimed by Kosovo Liberation Army.

Oct 1997
Serbian police allegedly beat around 350 people including students demonstrating about the non-implementation of the education agreement.

Nov 1997 on
Serbian operations intensify in Drenica, following clashes with the Kosovo Liberation Army. Ethnic Albanians report increase in serious human rights violations and violence by the police.

Feb-Aug 1998
Serbian operations leave hundreds of civilians dead, many apparently the result of deliberate or indiscriminate attacks. Over 180,000 people flee their homes.

Mass arrests followed. According to official figures, from 1981 to 1988 over 1,750 ethnic Albanians were sentenced by courts to up to 15 years' imprisonment for nationalist activities; another 7,000 were sentenced to up to 60 days' imprisonment for minor political offences.

In the late 1980s Slobodan Milošević came to power, first as President of the ruling League of Communists of Serbia and then President of Serbia (he is now the federal President), with a heavily Serbian nationalist programme which focused on Kosovo province. Serbian control over Kosovo would be reasserted by means of constitutional changes designed to limit the province's autonomy. In 1988 there were demonstrations throughout Serbia in support of this aim.

In February 1989 there was a general strike by ethnic Albanians in Kosovo province opposed to these constitutional changes. On 26 February, as the strike continued, the federal authorities decided to introduce 'special measures' – effectively a partial state of emergency. Key industries were put under compulsory work orders and large numbers of troops were brought into Kosovo province. On 23 March the Kosovo parliament under pressure from Serbia (tanks were stationed outside the parliament building at the time) approved the contested constitutional changes. These gave Serbia control of Kosovo's police, judiciary, civil defence, foreign relations and policy on official appointments. Further, Serbia acquired the right to make future constitutional changes without the consent of the province.

For more than a decade, Amnesty International has documented and campaigned against a systematic pattern of human rights violations in Kosovo province, including torture and ill-treatment by police, deaths in police custody, and unfair trials of political prisoners. The lack of effective redress for these and other violations of basic human rights in the province must be counted among the sources of frustration and anger which have culminated in the present conflict. A year-by-year summary follows with indicative cases.

1989

• In March at least 44 ethnic Albanians, among them prominent political and industrial leaders, were arrested in Kosovo for having allegedly incited unrest in the province in November 1988 and February 1989.

• Following the Kosovo Assembly's approval on 23 March of the contested constitutional amendments which gave the Republic of

Serbia greater powers over the province, there were six days of clashes between ethnic Albanian demonstrators and security forces in which, according to official figures, 24 people, two of them police officers, were killed and several hundreds wounded. Unofficial sources cite figures of over 100 deaths.

• Subsequently over 900 demonstrators, among them school pupils, were summarily sentenced to up to 60 days' imprisonment. Up to 2,000 miners and workers who refused compulsory work orders, or shop-workers who closed their shops in solidarity with strikers, were imprisoned for up to 60 days or were fined, dismissed or suspended from their jobs. Some 200 other people had their passports withdrawn.

• Purges of local members of the League of Communists of Kosovo, of journalists, teachers and others followed. In addition, between the end of March and July 1989, 237 ethnic Albanians, including people who had signed a petition against the constitutional changes, were arrested and held without charge in administrative detention.

1990

• Ethnic conflict intensified in Kosovo province. Between 24 January and 3 February there were further violent clashes in many parts of Kosovo between security forces and ethnic Albanian demonstrators calling for the resignation of local political leaders, the release of political prisoners and greater independence from Serbia. At least 30 ethnic Albanians died and several hundred others were injured. Over 1,000 ethnic Albanians who went on strike in support of the demonstrations or in other ways peacefully expressed nationalist dissent were imprisoned for up to 60 days.

• In July the Serbian parliament suspended the Kosovo government and parliament after ethnic Albanian members of the Kosovo parliament declared Kosovo independent of the Republic of Serbia. Thousands of ethnic Albanians who refused to declare their approval for the Serbian measures lost their jobs. The main local media in the Albanian language were banned, including the daily newspaper *Rilindja*.

• On 7 September ethnic Albanian deputies of the suspended Kosovo parliament met clandestinely and adopted a constitution proclaiming Kosovo a republic within the Yugoslav federation. At the end of September Serbia adopted a new constitution which deprived its two provinces of most of their autonomy. In December ethnic Albanians responded by boycotting Serbian elections. With the imposition of 'emergency measures' in most of the public sector of the economy, tens of thousands of Albanians were dismissed from their jobs, generally to be replaced by Serbs and Montenegrins.

1991

• Up to 6,000 ethnic Albanian secondary school teachers were dismissed from their posts, often for continuing to teach according to the curriculum laid down by the suspended Kosovo Council for Education instead of the curriculum set by the Serbian authorities. Over 800 ethnic Albanian teaching staff (amounting to 95 per cent of the total) were reportedly dismissed from Priština University. Classes with Albanian as the language of instruction were closed in almost all secondary schools and at the university in Priština. When teachers and students tried to return to classes they were frequently barred by police from entering.

In September 1991 an unofficial referendum was held by ethnic Albanians in Kosovo which supported the proposal that the province be proclaimed a sovereign and independent state with the right to take part in an eventual association of sovereign states within Yugoslavia.

1992

In April, following the break-up of the Socialist Federal Republic of Yugoslavia (SFRY), a new state, the Federal Republic of Yugoslavia (FRY), comprising the Republics of Serbia and Montenegro, was proclaimed in Belgrade. In May 1992, ethnic Albanians held their own elections in Kosovo province; these were not recognised as valid by Serbia.

Leaders of Kosovo's main ethnic Albanian political party, the Democratic League of Kosovo (LDK), now demanded Kosovo's full independence from Yugoslavia, a goal which they pledged to obtain by peaceful means. As tension in the province mounted, and with armed conflict raging in Bosnia-Herzegovina, the Conference on Security and Cooperation in Europe (CSCE) established in October 1992 a long-term mission in Kosovo to monitor the human rights situation.

• In Kosovo province, hundreds of ethnic Albanians were beaten or otherwise ill-treated by the police. Among the victims was Ismet Krasniqi (*see case at start of chapter*).

• From 1 September to 10 October ethnic Albanian sources alleged that 240 people (demonstrating against the closure of secondary schools and university faculties to ethnic Albanians) were beaten by police. Several hundred others were beaten during similar demonstrations on 12 to 13 October. Among those severely injured were Sabrie Rrustaj who had her ear torn off and suffered a broken arm, and Samile Pupovci who had her leg broken.

• At least 16 ethnic Albanians died after being shot by police in disputed circumstances. In one incident, Bajram Hoxhaj, Muharrem Hysenaj and Hasan Hysenaj died after being shot by police in the village of Uće on January 31. Ethnic Albanians alleged that police had arrested three school children and then opened fire on members of their families who sought their release.

• Ethnic Albanians continued to be sentenced to imprisonment for non-violent political activity. Among these were Shala and Behadin Krasniqi, sentenced for sending a cassette tape containing greetings for broadcast on a radio station in Albania.

1993

In July both the CSCE and the United Nations Special Rapporteur on Yugoslavia were refused permission by the Yugoslav Government to base monitoring missions of long duration in the Federal Republic of Yugoslavia. The authorities also refused visas to several human rights organisations, including Amnesty International. A wave of arrests of ethnic Albanians on political charges followed the departure of the CSCE mission from Kosovo.

• There were numerous reports of police ill-treatment and torture of ethnic Albanians. Political and human rights activists were often deliberately targeted. For example, Sami Kurteshi, an activist in the Council for the Defence of Human Rights and Freedoms, an ethnic Albanian human rights group, was arrested in July. He was taken to a police station where he was severely punched and beaten about the body with truncheons, including his genitals and the soles of his feet.

• Some 30 ethnic Albanians, sentenced to imprisonment for non-violent political activity, were recognised by Amnesty International as prisoners of conscience. For example, Hysen Matoshi, Naim Canaj and Muharrem Hoda were each imprisoned for 40 days for organising a concert to celebrate Albania's national day in November.

• Over 90 other ethnic Albanians were detained on charges of seeking the secession of Kosovo by violence. By the end of the year 18 of them had been sentenced to up to five years' imprisonment, often after unfair trials. Some had not used or advocated violence and were seen as prisoners of conscience by Amnesty International.

1994

- Over 250 people were detained for political reasons on charges of having sought to jeopardise Yugoslavia's territorial integrity by force of arms. Over 160 were ethnic Albanian former police employees, many of whom lawyers claimed had been severely tortured following arrest. One of them, Ramadan Ndrecaj, was admitted to hospital as a result of injuries inflicted by police.
- More than 90 ethnic Albanians, many of them activists for the Democratic League of Kosovo, were convicted in unfair trials. Some were seen as prisoners of conscience by Amnesty International. These included Ismail Kastrati, Sylejman Ahmeti and Mustafë Ibrahimi, who were sentenced to between two and two and a half years' imprisonment for founding a Chamber of Commerce, one of the 'parallel' institutions created by ethnic Albanians.
- Up to 2,000 people were ill-treated or tortured by police primarily for their ethnic identity. The majority of victims were ethnic Albanians. For example, Arian Curri (*see page* 69), a high school student, was arrested and beaten by police officers in Peć. One of them carved a Serbian symbol on his chest with a knife.
- Five men, four of them ethnic Albanians, died as a result of ill-treatment in police custody. One of these was Hajdin Bislami, who was arrested and beaten over three days by police who reportedly suspected his sons of having bought stolen goods. He was admitted to hospital and subsequently died.
- Ten ethnic Albanians were shot dead by police or soldiers, some in disputed circumstances. In some of these cases, it was clear that no officer was under attack. For example, Fidan Brestovci, aged six, died after being shot by a police officer while driving along with his family. A police statement said that the officer had mistaken the family car for that of a criminal. The officer was detained for investigation, but was reportedly released a month later pending trial.

1995

- Some 160 people, almost all ethnic Albanians, were sentenced to imprisonment on political charges after unfair trials. Many of these alleged that police officers had tortured them in order to extract false 'confessions'. Among them was Avdi Mehmedoviqi, a former police chief, who told the court that police beat him until he lost consciousness five or six times.

- Prisoners of conscience included at least 30 ethnic Albanians who were summarily sentenced to up to 60 days' imprisonment for holding 'illegal meetings'. Most of these were teachers who had held classes for ethnic Albanian students. They included Qazim Azemi, director of a high school in Vućitrn, who received three short prison sentences during the year.
- Several thousand ethnic Albanians were briefly detained for questioning about their political activities or alleged possession of arms. Many were considered prisoners of conscience by Amnesty International.
- There were widespread reports of torture and ill-treatment by police and at least four ethnic Albanians died in police custody. These included Shefki Latifi, political activist, who was arrested, beaten at the police station in Podujevo, and then released. He died a few hours later from a heart attack. A photograph of his body showed marks of heavy bruising on his back and buttocks, but a medical certificate recorded his death as natural and no police officer was charged with ill-treating him.
- Seven ethnic Albanians were shot dead by members of the security forces in disputed circumstances. One of these, Isa Berisha, a 10-year-old boy, was shot dead in the compound of a military barracks in Djeneral Janković. Military sources claimed that he had entered the compound to steal cigarettes, but his family claimed he was pursuing a stray goat. Proceedings were initiated against a soldier for 'violating patrol duties' in connection with the boy's death, but no charges appeared to have been brought by the end of the year.

1996

- Ethnic Albanian political leaders continued to call for independence by peaceful means. However, between April and October, nine Serbs were shot dead and six others were wounded. The KLA claimed responsibility. The attacks started after a young ethnic Albanian was shot dead by a Serb civilian in April.
- Torture and ill-treatment by police were widespread. Most victims were ethnic Albanians. At least two men died apparently as a result of torture by the police, and the deaths of two others appeared to be connected with police beatings. One such case concerned Feriz Blakçori, a school teacher, who died in hospital having been arrested by police the day before. His death certificate reportedly attributed his death to cardio-respiratory insufficiency due to severe shock caused by bruising to his head and body.

Ethnic Albanian woman with her grandson weeps in front of her burnt-out home in Rezalla village, after an offensive by Yugoslav army and Serb police (August 1998)

- Prisoners of conscience included over a dozen men sentenced to up to 60 days' imprisonment for peacefully exercising their right to freedom of assembly. They included Pal Krasniqi, who was imprisoned for holding a meeting of a school trade union branch.
- Around 60 political prisoners, ethnic Albanians, remained in prison, most of them convicted after unfair trials; some were possible prisoners of conscience.

1997

- Ethnic Albanian political parties continued to demand independence for Kosovo province by peaceful means. However, violent attacks against police stations, police officers, Serb civilians and ethnic Albanians working for or with the authorities occurred throughout the year. Responsibility for many of these attacks was claimed by a new organisation, the Kosovo Liberation Army (KLA). Police responses to the violence appeared to be indiscriminate arrests and house searches.

- Approximately 34 ethnic Albanian political prisoners were convicted, mostly after unfair trials. Scores of others remained in prisons. Some may have been prisoners of conscience. Among the most significant cases was that of Avni Klinaku and 19 other ethnic Albanians who were sentenced in Priština in May for 'conspiring to endanger the territorial integrity of the Federal Republic of Yugoslavia' and other similar charges. The trial was unfair: the conviction was based largely on self-incriminating statements which were not substantiated in court, and 11 of the accused alleged that the statements had only been given as a result of torture in custody.
- Detainees and peaceful demonstrators were routinely tortured or ill-treated by police. Most victims were ethnic Albanians from Kosovo province, but some were Serbs. Incidents in which police beat and ill-treated ethnic Albanians – including women, children and elderly people – took place almost daily throughout the year.
- At least three people, all ethnic Albanians, died in police custody. For example, Ismet Gjocaj died after being shot by police. Despite police claims that he had been shot while participating in an armed attack on a police station, there was clear evidence that at the time of his death he was already in custody and had been tortured.

1998

- On 28 February police reportedly clashed with members of the Kosovo Liberation Army in the village of Likošane, near Glogovac town. Two police officers and five Albanians, including one woman, were killed. Ethnic Albanians claim that at least seven, and possibly many more Albanians were shot dead by police firing from a helicopter in Cirez village the same day.
- On 2 March police broke up demonstration in Priština and other towns, using tear-gas, water cannons and truncheons. Sixteen ethnic Albanians and four police officers were reportedly killed during other clashes around the same time.
- Serbian authorities launch a succession of large-scale military operations against armed ethnic Albanian forces. Hundreds of civilians are killed in the ensuing fight for territory.

5

Human rights violated

'*They ordered my son to lie down then they searched him and ordered him to get up again and he did that. Again to lay down, they did not find anything, no weapons. I saw with my eyes how they prepared their automatic weapons, two of them, one on one side and another on the other, they shot him between the shoulders. I saw that with my eyes and screamed at that moment "Please God, I rely on you!" ... I didn't know what else I could say. I held those two walking sticks. I felt that my feet were completely cold. I could not feel them, I didn't know that they were mine.*'

Mother of 26-year-old **Nazmi Jashari**, killed by Serbian special police forces in Donji Prekaz on 5 March 1998.

Despite the fact that thousands of ethnic Albanians regularly witnessed or experienced violence at the hands of security forces, neither the Serbian nor the federal Yugoslav authorities have been willing to admit to the human rights concerns in Kosovo province. They have consistently failed to take action to prevent violations. This situation worsened after 1996 as the authorities sought ever more frequently to justify human rights violations by stating that they were operating against 'terrorists', and with the explosion of armed conflict it has now reached crisis point.

The most obvious targets of police violence have been ethnic Albanians who, by their political or other activity, are prominent in the organisation of the 'parallel' society that ethnic Albanians have created outside the official state structures. They include political activists, in particular members of the Democratic League of Kosovo (LDK); members of other ethnic Albanian political parties; teachers and academics; trade unionists; those involved in the organisation of humanitarian aid to families in need; even local sports leaders. Journalists, former police officers and former military also appear to be targeted.

However, police violence does not stop here. Its scope is much wider, affecting, for example, large numbers of families whose homes are searched by police for arms. The sense of insecurity this has provoked amongst ethnic Albanians, coupled with economic hardship and the fear of military call-up to the Yugoslav Army, have led several hundred thousands of ethnic Albanians, mainly young men, to leave the country. They have headed primarily for western Europe. The authorities' unstated policy appears to be to encourage their departure: most observers have concluded that the military authorities have not been systematically carrying out conscription in Kosovo, but rather using the threat of conscription as a means of inducing young men to leave the country. Similarly, the manner in which arms searches are carried out appears to be deliberately intended to intimidate, and has sometimes been accompanied by explicit threats to families to leave the country.

In March 1994 there were reports that western European governments might be considering the mass *refoulement* of asylum seekers from Yugoslavia (the majority of them ethnic Albanians). The authorities reacted by publicising their intention to prosecute all those who had fled the country to avoid military service (unless they consented to sign up on return) or who had deserted.

Ethnic Albanian human rights activists, members of the Council for the Defence of Human Rights and Freedoms in Priština, now report many incidents of police abuses every day. Brutal beatings with truncheons, punching and kicking are the most common forms of violence, but electric shocks have also sometimes been used by police officers. Police officers commonly express ethnic hatred towards their victims, who are verbally abused for being Albanian. Many victims have been so badly injured they have needed medical treatment or hospitalisation; several have died, apparently as a result of injuries they received from beatings.

Today, the scope and extent of human rights abuses in Kosovo is frightening. Violence can erupt in any form and for any reason. To live there is to expect the worst – on a daily basis. Amnesty International's detailed documentation on human rights violations in Kosovo province is here broken down into certain main categories of abuse.

Serbian policemen near a burning ethnic Albanian house near the village of Mališevo (July 1998)

Killings

From the end of February 1998 the marked increase in police and military actions in the areas where the KLA was reported to have a strong presence resulted in hundreds of killings. Many of these appear to have been extrajudicial executions. The deliberate killing of people taking no active part in hostilities contravenes minimum standards of human behaviour and is prohibited under the laws of armed conflict.

'This is what will happen next time, too...'

On 28 February and 1 March 1998 Serbian police killed 26 ethnic Albanians in the villages of Likošane and Cirez, in the Drenica area of Kosovo. Four police officers were also killed.

The police used helicopters and armoured vehicles in the operation, and were armed with machine guns and rocket-propelled grenades. It appears that although the KLA resisted, they were outnumbered and withdrew from the area, allowing the police to move in. Amnesty International believes that most of the ethnic Albanians who died were killed after the KLA's withdrawal.

Rukije Nebiu, a mother of two who was pregnant with her third child, was one of the 26 Albanian victims. She was killed in her house in Cirez village; pictures of her body indicated that she had been shot in the head with a high velocity weapon. Although Amnesty International holds photographic evidence of her body, it is considered too distressing to reproduce here. Rukije's husband Xhemsir Nebiu and her brother-in-law Ilir Nebiu were also shot in or close to the house. Other victims in Cirez included 63-year-old Ajet Rexhepi and four brothers from the Sejdiu family, including 24-year-old twins Nazmi and Bedri who were also reportedly found dead in their house.

Among others, 10 male members of the Ahmeti family, aged between 16 and 50 years, were killed in Likošane, apparently in extrajudicial executions. Mirsije Ahmeti, whose father and three brothers were killed, was reported in the Belgrade weekly *Vreme* as describing how the police came to their house at about 4pm on 28 February, ordered the occupants onto the floor at gunpoint, locked the women and children in one room and took the men out.[2] The men were at first believed to be missing and were apparently not counted in the 16 dead first reported by the police (the police in any case did not issue the names of the dead). On 2 March their bodies were seen in the morgue in Priština and they were returned to the village for burial on 3 March.

Visitors to the scene, including representatives of the Belgrade-based Humanitarian Law Centre (HLC)[3], observed and photographed blood, teeth and what they believed to be brain tissue on 1 March in the yard of the Ahmeti house. They also observed the words: 'This is what will happen next time, too' written in Serbian on the wall.

According to the HLC, 70-year-old Muhamet Djeli and his son Naser were killed in the house opposite that of the Ahmetis. Muhamet died in an outbuilding and Naser was shot in the next room in the presence of his wife and two children. He had been hit by a bullet which came through a window that had been covered with a mattress. A trail of blood indicated that he had been dragged outside, but his body was taken to the Priština morgue by police.

The HLC also reported that although many of the bodies were taken to the morgue, there were no signs that autopsies had been performed on them, nor on the bodies which were left in the village. To Amnesty International's knowledge, to date no investigations have been carried out into the killings.

---

[2] *Krvavi vikend u Drenici (Bloody weekend in Drenica)*, *Vreme*, Belgrade, 7 March 1998.
[3] *Investigations in Drenica*, 7 March 1998 and *Police Operations in the Drenica area*, 28 March 1998.

Unlawful deaths in custody

Until March 1998 and the police operations in Drenica (*see above and chapter 6*), most evidence of unlawful killings by police related to deaths in custody resulting from the torture and ill-treatment (and even shooting) of the victims during interrogation by police. The Council for the Defence of Human Rights and Freedoms (CDHRF) reported five such deaths in 1997. Two of these cases are described below.

Jonuz Zeneli was arrested on 30 April 1997 and was indicted in a group of 21 ethnic Albanians on charges of 'terrorism'. On 16 October 1997, shortly before the trial opened on 27 October, Jonuz Zeneli died in the hospital of the Belgrade Central Prison. He had been transferred there from the prison hospital in Kosovo province from where he had already complained of kidney pains to relatives as a result of torture and ill-treatment in detention. His relatives were reportedly not informed of the cause of his death by the police. A certificate issued by the prison hospital implied that he had died of lung cancer which had migrated to other parts of his body. However, photographs of the body showed indications of torture or ill-treatment and the circumstances point to this either being the cause of or a contributory factor in his death.

On 27 November 1997 Ismet Gjocaj was shot and killed by police in disputed circumstances in a village near Dećane. According to reports passed to the press by the police, he had been taking part in an armed attack on the police station in the village and had been killed by police returning fire. One police officer was reported to have been killed in the attack and another officer wounded. However, this account of Ismet Gjocaj's involvement in the attack does not appear credible. On 25 November Ismet Gjocaj had made a statement to the local CDHRF branch in Dećane, saying that on 21 November a police patrol had stopped and threatened him and another Albanian as they cut wood near the Albanian border. He said that he was then taken to his home which was searched, and that he and his brother were briefly detained and then told to report again to the police on 25 November (the day he gave the statement).

There is strong evidence that he had reported to the police and was in custody on the night of his death, which was when the reported attack on the police station occurred. A forensic pathologist consulted by Amnesty International, who examined photographs of Ismet Gjocaj's body, concluded that the body had freshly-inflicted multiple bruising, predominantly to the back, buttocks and arms. The bruising showed signs that it was inflicted with a baton, truncheon or similar object. Still more seriously, the majority of both the bruising and the bullet wounds had been inflicted from behind. The most likely explanation for Ismet Gjocaj's death is that he had been in custody at the time of the attack on the police station and that he was extrajudicially executed, possibly as a form of revenge for the reported death and injuries to police officers that night.

Torture and ill-treatment

'When they didn't find a gun, they said to me, "Give us the gun or we'll kill you". They didn't kill me, but they left my back, thighs and arms covered in bruises. They also put a rifle-butt between my legs but they didn't injure me... It's better that they beat me than my sons... It didn't last more than 20 to 35 minutes. Two or three times I felt dizzy from their blows, but I didn't lose consciousness, nor did I swear at them. I wasn't frightened, but I kept telling them that we didn't have a gun. We've hardly enough money for bread, much less a gun! But they swore at me and insulted me, and when they left they said they would be back for "the gun"!'

Shukrije Haxha from Brajina village near Podujevo, describing how three police officers carried out an arms search at her house on 31 July 1994 when her husband and sons were out.

The victims of police ill-treatment have often been political activists, journalists, human rights activists or teachers and students in the parallel education institutions. However, many people who are not active in these parallel institutions have also been victims, and their ill-treatment might be described as routine. Generally the worst instances of ill-treatment have occurred in police stations where it frequently amounted to torture.

Recently, hundreds of ethnic Albanians have been ill-treated during peaceful demonstrations in October and December 1997 in connection with education disputes and against police violence in the Drenica region in March 1998.

Violence during arms searches
A common scenario for the ill-treatment of ethnic Albanians is during

police raids on houses in villages, where police are ostensibly looking for hidden arms. Such searches became an everyday occurrence following the outbreak of armed conflict in the other parts of former Yugoslavia in 1991. Both illegally- and legally-held weapons were confiscated when found. Police ill-treatment occurred no matter whether arms were found or not. According to some reports the police even ordered people to purchase a weapon to hand over when none were found. Men were often also detained by police whether or not a weapon was found, and female family members were sometimes ill-treated, or intimidated by the police officers' violent behaviour.

Many of the areas where the arms searches were most intense, such as the area bordering Albania, were the scene of major security forces operations and clashes with the KLA in mid-1998. Such arms searches as described here are probably now less frequent but have been replaced by even more serious scenarios, such as that in Likošane (*see under* Killings *above*), where police went in pursuit of armed men and their actions resulted in possible extrajudicial executions. The arms searches nevertheless form a significant part of the context to today's situation in Kosovo province.

Traumatised victim

Qamil Xhemajli was arrested in the early hours of 31 January 1997. He had been targeted and harassed by police before, probably because he and other members of his extended family had already been imprisoned on political charges in the past and four of them had fled abroad.

'... the police surrounded our house ... they began to break down the door, so I quickly opened it. They immediately asked me if I was Qamil and handcuffed me. They asked me where I kept illegal materials and where I had hidden the arms which had been used to kill police officers. When I denied possessing any of this, they began to punch me in the face and body. They searched the bookshelves and broke up furniture in the house. They found only family photographs, letters from prison and some cassette tapes with songs — nothing else. They then took me to the house of my brother Bajrush, who is in prison serving a sentence. Only his wife, Shahadija, and two small children, were there. After they had searched the house, they took away some family photographs. Then they took me into the field asking me who owned the land and woods and what was hidden there. Later they led me back to my house and began to punch me in the face and again demanded that I hand over documents and arms. Other officers were searching the woods and farmyard.'

Qamil Xhemajli was later chained to a metal cupboard in the police station in Uroševac and beaten by police trying to make him confess to killing a police officer, possessing arms and being a member of a clandestine organisation. After a day and a half he was transferred to prison and was beaten further by police before being released. A doctor's examination some two weeks later confirmed that he had a broken rib and still had bruises to his head and body. Such incidents of torture also have a traumatising effect on the victim's relatives. Qamil Xhemajli's mother said: 'When he came home he could hardly walk. He was half dead ... he was like a shadow, you couldn't recognise him. The children wouldn't go near him, they ran away from him.' Qamil Xhemajli himself interpreted this and other visits by police and summonses to report to them as being intended to intimidate his family into leaving, claiming that: 'They even said to me once: "What are you doing here, go to Switzerland or we'll kill you. You're either stupid or crazy to remain in Kosovo".'

Unfair trials

The Serbian authorities have consistently failed to ensure fair trials in political cases. Some 34 people were convicted and imprisoned in three major political trials in 1997 and another 16 people were convicted in absentia in the same trials. More criminal proceedings in similar cases are in process in 1998 and there may be many more unfair political trials to come.

The cases of torture and ill-treatment described above illustrate what happens to the majority of victims — those who are ill-treated outside of police stations or detained or held by police even for relatively brief periods. The consequences for those who are detained for longer periods and subsequently put on trial can be even more serious: victims are coerced into making statements incriminating themselves or others which are subsequently accepted as evidence in court[4]. Beyond the use of such testimony, Amnesty International is concerned

---

[4] This practice is in violation of Article 15 of the UN Convention against Torture, which requires that '...any statement which is established to have been made as a result of torture shall not be invoked as evidence in any proceedings, except against a person accused of torture as evidence that the statement was made.' Furthermore, the UN Special Rapporteur on Torture has underscored the role of the judiciary in ensuring this rule is respected and thereby preventing torture. (EICN.4/1992/17, page 103, paragraph 280)

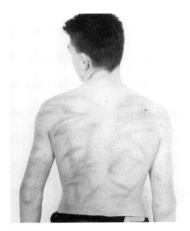 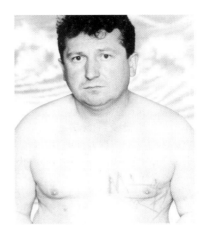

'Routine' torture and ill-treatment

On 2 September 1997 plainclothes police officers came to the home of 16-year-old Fërdian Ibërdemaj (*above left*) in Peć accusing him of stealing a bicycle. He was taken out of the town to the hills near Brestovik village, held there for several hours and beaten before being left there. Examination of photographs of his injuries by a pathologist confirmed injuries consistent with him having been beaten with flexible truncheons or rubber pipes.

On 12 April 1998, 38-year-old Soko Rugovac (*above right*), a Muslim from the town of Rozaj in Montenegro, some 40 kilometres north of Peć, was stopped by police in Peć while taking a taxi from the bus station to his aunt's house. According to statements he later gave to the Montenegrin police and press, he was ordered out of the taxi without any apparent reason, driven to the main police station and taken straight to the basement. They first asked him if he had come to Pec to participate in the ethnic Albanians' demonstration the next day, and then if he had come 'to buy votes for Milo Djukanović' at the Montenegrin parliamentary elections that were held in May.[5] When he admitted that he had voted for Djukanović in the presidential elections, the two police officers branded the letters MILO on his chest with a hot soldering iron, cut lines on his chest with a knife and punched and slapped him. Following the incident the Montenegrin Ministry of the Interior issued a protest to its Serbian equivalent calling for action against the police officers involved. The Belgrade newspaper *Vreme* reported on 25 April that the Peć police station had claimed that the whole story was invented by the Montenegrin police.

---

[5] Milo Djukanović is the Montenegrin president who was elected in December 1997 and is in conflict with the Serbian and Federal authorities and with the Federal President and former Serbian President, Slobodan Milošević, in particular.

about numerous reported violations of the Yugoslav Federal Code of Criminal Procedure (CCP) and international standards. Here victims are detained arbitrarily without due process, including violation of their right to communicate freely with a defence lawyer.

The situation in law

The charges applied in political cases against ethnic Albanians are usually based on the Federal Criminal Code, which excludes the possibility of the death penalty, having substituted a maximum 20-year prison sentence in its place. The death penalty is possible for 'aggravated murder' under the Serbian Criminal Code.

In Article 196, the CCP specifies that the police can only detain suspects for a maximum of three days, and then only in exceptional circumstances such as for the purposes of verifying alibis. Police detention should not be a usual part of the judicial process. The police are normally required to inform and hand over the suspect to the investigating magistrate, who will supervise the investigations while the suspect is detained in an investigatory prison. International standards such as the UN Body of Principles for the Protection of All Persons under Any Form of Detention or Imprisonment specify that a detainee should be entitled to communicate freely with his or her legal counsel, and that this right can only be suspended in exceptional circumstances, and then only for a matter of days. These rights are laid down both as a safeguard against torture or ill-treatment and to ensure fair trials. The CCP, however, does not guarantee this right while detainees are in police custody, despite the fact that both the Federal and Serbian Constitutions (Articles 29 and 24, respectively) specify that 'everyone has the right to be interrogated in the presence of defence counsel of his choice'.

The situation in practice

The CCP is routinely abused. Suspects are held for the three days and frequently for much longer without being passed into the custody of an investigating magistrate. Defence lawyers allege that police also continue to interrogate detainees after their transfer to investigatory prisons. It is of particular concern that it is during this period that ill-treatment by police takes place. In the case of those suspected of more serious crimes such as terrorism, this often amounts to torture to extract statements by coercion. Without access to lawyers, detainees are not given the opportunity of 'necessary expert assistance' to appeal against the detention according to Article 196 of the CCP. Even more seriously, Articles 10 and 218, paragraph 8 of the CCP, which explicitly prohibit the extraction of statements from suspects or witnesses by use of force or threats, are routinely ignored during investigatory proceedings.

Suspects are thus typically detained – without access to defence lawyers, family or doctors – for days, or sometimes even weeks, while police interrogate them using various methods of torture aimed at forcing them to sign 'confessions' incriminating themselves and/or others. The forms of torture and ill-treatment appear to consist of combinations of beatings with fists, truncheons, rubber pipes or other blunt objects. In some cases electric shock batons are used as well as beating. The police have tortured suspects using electric shock batons to minimise any visible signs of torture or ill-treatment which would otherwise result from beatings or similar physical stress.

Even after transfer to investigatory prisons, defence lawyers are normally denied the opportunity to communicate freely and in confidence with their clients as required by the Body of Principles and the General Comment of the UN Human Rights Committee on Article 14 (3) of the International Covenant on Civil and Political Rights (ICCPR)[6]. The CCP allows investigating magistrates to restrict communication between defendants and their defence lawyers before the indictment has been issued, or the investigations have been completed, without any checks or balances on this restriction (Article 74). In practice, defendants are also often denied free communication after the indictment has been issued.

Unfair trials in 1997

The concerns cited above are illustrated by three political trials which were held in 1997. Between October 1996 and February 1997 Serbian police arrested over 100 people in connection with investigations into armed attacks against Serbian police and civilians during 1996. The bulk of the arrests were made in January 1997.

---

[6] In its General Comment 13 (Article 14, Twenty-first session, 1984) the Human Rights Committee stated that 14(3) (b) of the ICCPR '...requires counsel to communicate with the accused in conditions giving full respect for the confidentiality of their communications. Lawyers should be able to counsel and to represent their clients in accordance with their established professional standards and judgement without any restrictions, influences, pressures or undue interference from any quarter.' (HRI/GEN/1, page 15, paragraph 9)

Some of the suspects were held incommunicado for many days: Besim Rama and Avni Nura were detained by police on 17 September 1996, but despite continuous efforts their family and defence lawyers were unable to obtain information about their whereabouts until early October. Then in early October, after at least 13 days' interrogation by police during which they allege they were tortured, the men were questioned by investigating magistrates. In the indictment their custody was recorded as having commenced on 29 September. Their lawyers were not allowed to be present during this interrogation. Only on 8 October were the lawyers able to visit their clients and even then were not able to speak freely with them and discuss the charges against them. In addition Besim Rama's brother, Osman Rama, stated that he was bundled into a car by plainclothes police officers and taken to an unknown location where he was beaten and questioned about Besim's political activities. He was released and detained again for a further six days' interrogation during which he was tortured before being released.

At least 100 people were arrested in January and February 1997. Thirty-five of these were subsequently tried and two, Besnik Restelica and Jonuz Zeneli [*see under* Killings, *above*], died in custody. There were reports that most had been tortured or ill-treated during their detention and interrogation. One of the worst cases was represented by Nait Hasani who was arrested on 28 January 1997. On 29 January he was transferred by police to a hospital in Priština, reportedly because he was in a coma as a result of the beatings he had received from the police. His family then found on 31 January that he had been abducted from the hospital. Despite their efforts to obtain information from the police about his whereabouts, the authorities denied any involvement with his abduction. He reappeared on 28 February when he was brought before an investigating magistrate and questioned in the presence of his defence lawyer. His lawyer later reported that his client had told him that he had been taken by police to an unknown location where he was tied to a bed, tortured with electric shocks and ill-treated in other ways, with the aim of forcing him to sign incriminating 'confessions'.

Those arrested between October 1996 and February 1997 were subsequently indicted in three groups which came to trial between May and December 1997. The first of these is described below.

The trial of Avni Klinaku and 17 others
In May 1997 Avni Klinaku, 15 other ethnic Albanian men and two

women were sentenced to prison for between two and 10 years. Another two men were convicted in absentia at the same trial. The charges against them were various combinations of Article 136 of the Federal Criminal Code (association for the purpose of hostile activity) and Article 116 (endangering the territorial integrity of the Federal Republic of Yugoslavia). Six of them, including Avni Klinaku himself, were also convicted under Article 125 (terrorism). They were accused of forming or belonging to a clandestine organisation called the National Movement for the Liberation of Kosovo (NMLK) whose aim was allegedly to attempt, by the use of force, to detach Kosovo province and other areas of Yugoslavia inhabited by ethnic Albanians and form a separate state which would unite with Albania. Five were accused of having planned and prepared for an armed attack on a police patrol, and another four were accused of having handled arms. The others were mostly accused of having produced or distributed the organisation's newspaper *Çlirimi* ('Liberation') or having recruited members to the organisation. Many of the defendants denied that they had been involved in terrorism and 10 claimed that they had done no more than distribute *Çlirimi*. Five denied that they had even been members of the organisation.

At the trial, 11 of the defendants submitted statements to the effect that they had been tortured or ill-treated during interrogation and that they had given statements under duress. According to the Belgrade-based Humanitarian Law Centre (HLC), the defendant Emin Salahu described in detail how he was tortured before he gave his statement: 'a gas mask was placed over his face, paper was pushed into his mouth, he was beaten with rubber and electric clubs on the hands, legs and kidney areas and threatened with the administration of drugs.'[7] In the written judgment the judge recorded that Emin Salahu 'did not want to give his defence because the statements ... were the result of the application of coercion, force and violence against him'. Other defendants similarly retracted their statements in court, although the written judgment recorded only three of them as having complained of torture (Enver Dugolli, for example, complained of torture[8], but his complaint was not recorded in the written judgment). Statements extracted under torture during the initial period of interrogation were

---

[7] HLC Communique, *Pristina court rules without evidence*, 2 June 1997.
[8] Cited in *Two trials of Kosovo Albanians charged with offences against the State in the Federal Republic of Yugoslavia in 1997*, document of the United Nations High Commission for Human Rights (E/CN.4/1998/9).

apparently presented and accepted by the court as some of the most substantial evidence for the prosecution.

A report by Elisabeth Rehn, then UN Commission of Human Rights Special Rapporteur responsible for the former republic of Yugoslavia, which was based on the observations of her field officers at the time of the trial, found numerous other violations of international standards of fair trial[9]. According to some of the defence lawyers, two lay members sitting on the bench with the judges were retired police officers, thus undermining the appearance of independence and impartiality of the court. More significantly, the defendants were denied an adequate opportunity to prepare their defence. Defence lawyers were denied access to almost all relevant trial documents until two weeks before the trial commenced. In addition, according to the UN report, some of the defendants only gained defence lawyers after they entered court at the opening of the trial. Those who had defence lawyers before the trial were not in any case able to communicate with them in private as guards were always in earshot. Defendants were thus not even free to complain to their lawyers of the torture and ill-treatment they said they had suffered.

According to the HLC no witness testimony was presented (other than the examination of the defendants themselves) and the only non-documentary evidence was one machine gun. When challenged by the defence lawyers to produce other weapons allegedly possessed, the prosecution admitted that no others had been found; they figured in the defendants' 'confessions' only. The judgment nevertheless recorded them as having possessed the weapons. Documentary evidence, in addition to the NMLK statute and copies of *Çlirimi*, reportedly also consisted of photocopies and police lists of objects found in searches.

Although some defendants admitted parts of the charges, such as membership of the NMLK and producing and distributing *Çlirimi*, others denied the substance of the charges in total. For example, Shukrije Rexha was recorded in the judgment as stating that three articles written by her had appeared in *Çlirimi*, but that she had had little contact with the editors and had not had time to learn of the nature of the organisation.

Further concerns stem from the fact that nearly eight months passed between the issuing of the verdicts in court on 30 May 1997 and the receipt of the written judgment by the defence lawyers on 31 January

---

[9] *ibid.*

A family with horsecart loaded with household belongings, takes refuge in the forest with thousands of ethnic Albanians who fled from Rakovici in Drenica (August 1998)

1998. Although, in accordance with international standards, the initial trial was held and concluded promptly, the defendants have been hugely delayed in their opportunity to submit appeals which had to await the written judgment. No investigations are known to have been initiated into the defendants' allegations of extraction of statements by means of torture.

As of late May 1998 there were dozens of other ethnic Albanians in detention in similar political cases, some of whom have been indicted. Amnesty International is seeking details of these detainees amid fears that they too have been tortured or ill-treated in custody and will face unfair trials.

Families under threat

Until the escalation of violence in the current conflict, the most widely experienced form of police violence in Kosovo province was that undergone by families during police searches for arms. These became a prominent feature of policing in Kosovo after the outbreak of armed conflict in the former Yugoslavia in 1991. Since 1997 arms searches have increased dramatically, and are now conducted on a daily basis, most intensively in border villages and rural areas, but also more generally throughout the province.

Legal and illegal possession of arms is widespread in Kosovo province, as elsewhere in the Federal Republic of Yugoslavia. Many reports state that during these raids police have confiscated not only illegal weapons (generally revolvers and hunting rifles), but also arms for which the owner possesses a licence. In other cases, families have been forced to hand over money or valuables to police or police have confiscated individual passports.

Because of the traditional pattern of settlement in rural areas of Kosovo, in which large extended families tend to live together, police raids are normally witnessed and personally experienced by many relatives. The sense of insecurity they provoke is further exacerbated by the pervasive presence in the province of the Yugoslav Army, and by the belief, strongly held by ethnic Albanians, that local Serbian communities have not only been spared these searches but have actually been given arms by the authorities.

Accounts of arms searches in the Albanian-language press or from other ethnic Albanian sources repeatedly refer to the deliberately intimidating and destructive way in which they are conducted: furniture is broken up, the inmates of the house are threatened, shouted and sworn at, and the men of the house are frequently arrested and beaten in local police stations or, even more humiliatingly, in their homes in front of their families. These beatings are often severe, causing injuries: reports of the victim losing consciousness as a result of beating, or of suffering bruising, broken teeth or ribs, are not uncommon. It is not only those found to possess unlicensed arms who are at risk of being beaten: those who do not possess weapons may also find themselves bearing the brunt of police frustration. The principle of 'guilt by association' seems often to apply: police officers unable to find a specific man they are looking for are frequently reported to have instead arrested or beaten a member of his family. While most police violence is directed against adult males, in some cases the elderly, women or children who are members of the family are not spared beatings. There have also been cases in which police have explicitly arrested a family member as a hostage in order to force a relative to give himself up to police. Some families have been repeatedly searched; under such a barrage of harassment, at times accompanied by threats such as 'Get out of here' or 'Go to Albania', many individuals and even whole families have opted to leave the country.

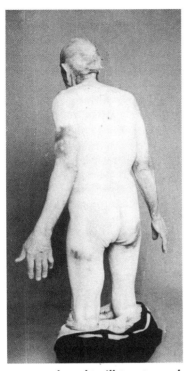

The beating of a 90-year-old man

Ali Murat Murati, aged 90, from Donja Lapašćtica village near Podujevo, was beaten by police who carried out an arms search at his home on 11 February 1994. According to his statement:

'At about 3pm, 15 or 16 police officers and two state security officers from Priština suddenly arrived in three police NIVA jeeps and an official car. A number of them surrounded our locality, carrying their arms at the ready to fire into my courtyard. At [the family's] old house four or five police officers and two state security officers began to carry out a search and to ill-treat members of the family... They took hold of me as I was standing on the staircase of the old house with members of my family and led me some 50 to 60 metres away into the new house. As soon as they brought me inside, they began to threaten me in the most brutal way, demanding that I hand over weapons, pistols, guns, automatic rifles. I told them repeatedly that I did not possess any arms and they could carry out a detailed search. They began to beat me in the most violent way, one after another, five or six of them, without stopping, until 4.30pm... I lost consciousness. The medical examination, certificate and photographs... are proof that they caused me severe bodily injuries and endangered my life.'

The agony of 'disappearances'

Article 7 of the UN Declaration on the Protection of All Persons from Enforced Disappearance, adopted by General Assembly Resolution 47/133 of 18 December 1992, states that: 'No circumstances whatsoever, whether a threat of war, a state of war, internal political instability or any other public emergency, may be invoked to justify enforced disappearances.' Article 13 of the Declaration requires that prompt investigations be initiated whenever there are reasonable grounds to believe that an enforced disappearance has occurred.

It is still too early to ascertain accurate statistics for 'missing' or 'disappeared' ethnic Albanians. The confusion resulting from the massive displacement of families driven from their homes by fear of attack or by attack itself and unable to maintain contact with one another means that all figures need to be treated with caution. However, Albanian sources have given the figure of around 500 ethnic Albanians whose 'disappearance' they lay at the door of the authorities. The United Nations High Commission for Refugees (UNHCR) gave a total of 400 gathered during its registration of those reported as unaccounted for. The UNHCR believes that around 200 of these are currently in police detention.

It is equally difficult to be precise about the number of those who have gone 'missing' at the hands of the Kosovo Liberation Army. On 3 August the Serbian Media Centre in Priština reported that in the period between 1 January and 27 July 1998, the KLA had been responsible for the 'kidnap' of 171 people, 37 of whom had been released, seven had escaped, and 15 killed. On 6 August Beatrice Weber, the Priština representative of the International Committee of the Red Cross (ICRC) stated that the organisation was investigating the cases of 138 Serbs and Montenegrins reportedly abducted by the KLA, and over 400 Albanians reportedly detained by Serbian forces.

It is not always possible to ascribe responsibility for the abduction of the 'disappeared' or 'missing' person beyond doubt. There are sometimes no witnesses to the events, for many of those who are being sought have vanished en route, setting off to visit relatives or to go to work, but never arriving at their destination. Others have refused to leave their homes when others flee, and then are not seen again. This is yet another burden for their relatives to bear, for although they may suspect one side or the other to be responsible, they can never be quite sure, and do not know with any certainty where to turn for help.

In some cases, bodies have been buried unidentified, leaving the relatives of those unaccounted for fearing that it is their loved one who is lying in an unmarked grave, yet still hoping that they are alive, and may yet reappear. Since there is a clear pattern of behaviour by the Serbian police and courts whereby ethnic Albanians are detained, and then held in unacknowledged detention for a lengthy period until finally appearing in court, their relatives can never be sure what may be the fate of their missing father or mother, brother or sister, son or daughter, husband or wife.

However, there are some cases where there are reports of their arrest. For example, the Council for the Defence of Human Rights and Freedoms (CDHRF) reported that Dr Hafir Shala, a physician at the Medical Centre of Glogovac, was arrested by police on 10 April 1998. The car in which he was travelling was stopped by police at about 8am in the village of Slatina near Priština and he and his two companions were arrested. According to statements by these companions, they were driven to the police headquarters in Priština by uniformed police, whereas Hafir Shala was driven there in a separate vehicle said to be occupied by three men in civilian clothes. This vehicle was seen to enter the station. Although Hafir Shala's companions were released later that day after questioning, he himself was not. No information concerning his whereabouts has been released by the authorities, despite efforts by his family and lawyer. By June, the authorities had reportedly denied that Hafir Shala was being held in custody at all.

Eight men 'disappear' from Novi Poklek

Ahmet Berisha	40 years
Hajriz Hajdini	48 years
Muhamet Hajdini	45 years
Sahit Qorri	60 years
Sefer Qorri	55 years
Ferat Hoti	39 years
Rama Asllani	60 years
Blerim Shishani	15 years

Novi Poklek is a settlement which was built in recent years on the edge of Glogovac. On 31 May 1998 a large operation was mounted by the police in and around the settlement.

Earlier that morning there had reportedly been an incident in which a police officer (apparently off duty and in a civilian vehicle) was involved in a car crash. No other vehicles were involved in the incident.

Whether the crash happened because the car was fired at or for other reasons cannot be ascertained.

It is alleged that nine or more men were killed during the subsequent police operation. Despite the lack of confirmed information, eight men who were reportedly detained by the police remain unaccounted for.

On the afternoon of 31 May at about 1pm a large force of police arrived in several dozen vehicles at the outskirts of the settlement. The police then began firing on houses in the settlement from the vehicles, positions near them and from buildings on the edge of Glogovac which lay only a few hundred metres from Novi Poklek. After about half an hour, patrols of police started to go from house to house in the settlement, ordering the inhabitants out of the buildings. Many of them were reportedly collected in a house in the settlement where men were separated from women and children. The women and children were directed to walk to the nearby village of Vasiljevo. Eight of the men who were reported to have been separated from them remain unaccounted for.

The bodies of two other men, Ardian Deliu (18) and Fidai Shishani (17), were reportedly found at the scene, but it has not yet been possible to establish the circumstances of their death.

There have been various reports about the fate of the missing men, including claims that bodies or body parts have been seen in the village; that the police were seen apparently transporting prisoners in the direction of the Feronikl factory where they are being held, or that they have been killed and buried in a mass grave. On 11 June a group of lawyers from Priština, who have been given power of attorney by relatives of the missing men, addressed a letter to the Serbian and Federal judicial authorities and police claiming that nine men had been killed and asking for an investigation into the incident, for the bodies to be located, an autopsy to be performed on them, and for the bodies to be handed over to the relatives for burial. The letter has been acknowledged by the district court, but no other replies had been received from the authorities by the end of June.

Political activists at risk

'During the interrogation they kept hitting me with a rubber truncheon on my hands, hitting first one hand 10-13 times and then the other, causing me internal bleeding (bruising)

which covered the palms and back of both hands and also the region of the forearms for which I have as evidence a medical certificate and photographs...'

A young woman, **Shqipe Sejdiu,** a human rights activist from Uroševac, arrested in January 1994 for attending a concert (described below).

Among the most frequent targets of police violence are political activists, in particular members of the LDK. However, there are also frequent reports of police harassment or ill-treatment of members of other ethnic Albanian political parties. Former political prisoners, human rights activists, trade unionists, former police officers and former military men also appear to be particularly targeted. Prisoners of conscience include ethnic Albanians sentenced to up to 60 days imprisonment for offences such as organising meetings or holding classes outside the official Serbian system. Amnesty International does not always have full details of the charges against the accused and the evidence in support of them. However, it appears that at least some of those detained are prisoners of conscience – that is people imprisoned because of their peaceful political activity – and that charges of belonging to clandestine organisations seeking to change Kosovo's status by force are not convincingly substantiated in court.

The Uroševac concert

A well-documented incident occurred on 31 January 1994 in Uroševac at a concert in privately-owned premises. It was held to commemorate five ethnic Albanian nationalist leaders, who had died violently in clashes with the police in Kosovo or were killed abroad, many suspect by agents working for the state security service. The organisers and audience included former political prisoners, human rights activists and political activists, including chairpersons or members of local LDK branches.

After the concert finished and the public was dispersing, police arrested some 40 people and took them to the local police headquarters. Here they were held for up to nine hours, interrogated and all allegedly beaten, often very brutally, by police and officers of the state security police (SDB). One of those arrested, who wishes to remain unnamed, has alleged that he was sexually assaulted by a senior police officer.

Rexhep Ismani, chairman of an artists' club in Uroševac and one of the members of a committee which organised the concert, wrote the

Yugoslav soldiers load a helicopter with weapons captured in fighting between Yugoslav border guards and ethnic Albanian arms smugglers on Mt Djeravica (July 1998)

following statement on 4 February 1994:

'At the end of the concert word went round that police were taking the registration numbers of cars of those attending the concert. The audience began quietly to depart, and the Organising Committee and other activists and guests went to the reception room of our host where a meal was prepared. As the guests were seated word came that the building was surrounded. The doors remained closed and a silence settled on those present. Then the bell rang and armed inspectors and police came in...They started to carry out an identity check...As I was near the door I was among the first to be ordered to go downstairs where other police were waiting.' He and some 15 others were put into a police van and taken to local police headquarters, where they were greeted by shouts and insults. 'They lined us up with our face to the wall, and took us one by one into an office to take down our names and addresses.

'They then took us up to the second floor to an open corridor where they began to beat us in the most brutal manner. One police officer with a shaved head, who changed his truncheon for a larger one which he held in both hands, beat us with all his might... A number of police officers came and joined him and in a frenzy began collectively to kick and punch us and beat us with truncheons, aiming at vital parts of the body, such as the head, kidneys, legs, back and hands.

'With our faces turned to the wall they continued to beat us until we were fainting or bleeding from our injuries... After six hours of beatings, threats and insults, they used warm water to revive those who had lost consciousness. Afterwards the interrogations started on the third floor.' Rexhep Ismani was asked who had organised the concert, what songs and poems had been recited, who had made the sets.

'After they had taken down my statement they led me down to a prison cell where I found Xhabir, Syle and Ilmi [who had been arrested at the same time]. We spent the night in pain in damp, cold surroundings smelling of urine. We spent the whole night on our feet until dawn broke... At 2.30pm they sent us to the court for petty offences...' The trial was postponed.

Demonstrators shot and beaten

On 18 March 1998 thousands of ethnic Albanians attempted to demonstrate in Peć. Many of those were coming into the town from villages in the area, particularly those on the plain to the east of the town. The police blocked the road close to the railway line on the east side of town and a large crowd of demonstrators wanting to enter the town from the villages accumulated there. Around 11am Qerim Muriqi (aged 50) was killed by a shot fired into the crowd. Witnesses believed that the shot came from an adjacent apartment block but did not see the gunman himself. Following Qerim Muriqi's shooting the crowd became very agitated and at some point some members of the crowd started to throw stones at the line of police which was blocking them. The police on the ground then fired into the crowd using both automatic fire and single shots, although by some accounts they may have first fired into the air. As the firing started most of the crowd tried to flee, but many were caught and beaten by the police. At least five people received bullet wounds.

From the witnesses' accounts of the incident Amnesty International can find no justification for the police's use of firearms at the demonstration. It is clear that they should have had some crowd control methods other than firearms once some individuals had started throwing stones. The UN Basic Principles on the Use of Force and Firearms by Law Enforcement Officials puts explicit limitations on the use of firearms, stating that: 'Law enforcement officials shall not use firearms against persons except in self-defence or defence of others against the imminent threat of death or serious injury, to prevent the perpetration of a particularly serious crime involving great threat to life, to arrest a person presenting such a danger and resisting their authority, or to prevent his or her escape, and only when less extreme means are insufficient to achieve these objectives. In any event, intentional lethal use of firearms may only be made when strictly unavoidable in order to protect life' (Article 9).

Amnesty International has observed that the police regularly place snipers at vantage points at demonstrations. It is clear that the authorities should at the very minimum investigate the circumstances of the killing and wounding of demonstrators and hold to account anyone responsible for violating international standards and national law on the use of lethal force.

Amnesty International delegates who visited Peć three days after the incident interviewed eight men and four women who stated that they had been beaten (most of them had visible signs of this), four men who had been shot and other witnesses who confirmed details of the shootings and beatings. The CDHRF reported[10] that 97 people were injured as a result of beatings that day. The testimony collected by Amnesty International in just one part of the town indicates that this

Sixteen-year-old schoolgirl recalls attack

'We gathered at our meeting point and then suddenly we were told to disperse. We started to run away and the ones who were behind us, mainly women, fell over. I tumbled over as well, and I was completely lost because I did not know what to do. They were shooting around us with machine guns, then this guy came near and pulled me away. After that another boy picked me up and took me all the way to his house. I relaxed there for a while and then we realised that the policemen were coming into the house. We locked ourselves in a room and then we saw another man coming in who was locking the front door. But the policemen were able to break the door and enter the room where we were. There were four policemen, and we were four women and another man who managed to escape. We were trapped. When they started to beat the others I was hiding behind an armchair. I got very frightened. They threw the others out; meanwhile two policemen directed their machine guns towards my head saying: "Stand up!" I was really scared and stood up because I just had to. They beat me with the end of a truncheon and I could see blood coming out of me. ... Then the women of the house picked me up and put me into the kitchen and I dragged myself behind the door. They were beating the others, pushing them out and then they realised that it was me who was missing and they said: "There is another blonde girl here". They began searching for me everywhere, when this fat policeman opened the door and saw me hiding. I said to him in Serbian: "I know Serbian, please don't hit me. Do you have children at home? Don't you see that I'm young?" Then they asked me how old I was, I said I was 16. Within a minute someone shouted: "One, two, three, out!" and they all went out. However, as this policeman was leaving he hit me once more around my neck and I know that I lost consciousness then.'

Merita, 16, describing what happened to her following a demonstration in Peć on 18 March 1998 number represents an accurate picture of what happened. The victims were not just beaten at the location near the railway line where the police stopped the gathering demonstrators, but also in the surrounding area. Some were beaten in houses where they had taken shelter.

Dangers in education

According to reports published in Rilindja on 14 and 15 February 1994, police arrested Tafil Brahimaj, director of a primary school in Kraljane village near Djakovica, on 9 February. Officers of the state security police (SDB) in Djakovica interrogated him about the school's curriculum and also asked him for a gun. When he denied possessing any weapon, they burned him by forcing him to sit on a heated stove. He was then released and ordered to report again to the SDB in Djakovica in 10 days time. Tafil Brahimaj was obliged to seek medical treatment for his injuries.

In 1990 and 1991 the Serbian authorities introduced a uniform curriculum throughout the whole of the Republic of Serbia and abolished the province's educational authority. The total number of enrolments in secondary Albanian-language schools was drastically reduced and a considerable number of educational institutions were closed. Many subjects at Priština University were no longer taught in the Albanian language but only in Serbian. More than 18,000 ethnic Albanian teachers and other staff in Albanian-language schools and the university who refused to recognise these changes and follow the new curriculum were dismissed. Instead they created a parallel educational system, using the old curricula, and lessons began to be held in private homes.

The issue of education has thus become one of the key points of confrontation in Kosovo. The Serbian authorities have systematically harassed those involved in the educational process, including members of the teachers' trade union, teachers, university lecturers, private citizens who have made their homes available for teaching and even pupils themselves. Schools have been broken into and raided, teachers arrested and/or beaten and lessons repeatedly interrupted. The Serbian authorities closed and sequestrated the Academy of Sciences and Arts of Kosovo and the Institute of Albanian Studies, regarded by ethnic Albanians as the bastions of Albanian culture and by the Serbian

---

[10] CDHRF Weekly Report 400, 22 March 1998

Law students in the underground Albanian university in Priština (March 1998)

authorities as hotbeds of secessionist aspirations.

In August 1993, the Humanitarian Law Fund, a human rights organisation based in Belgrade, published a report on human rights violations in Kosovo province and concluded: 'The investigation conducted by the Humanitarian Law Fund in the latter half of June 1993 indicates that the authorities of the Republic of Serbia, since the suspension and abolition of the Kosovo educational system, apply different forms of pressure and coercion against all those taking part in, or supporting, the autonomous Albanian schooling system'. Other independent observers have come to similar conclusions.

Demonstrations violently broken up

In October 1997 the leaders of the independent students union of ethnic Albanians from the parallel university in Priština initiated a series of peaceful demonstrations demanding access to the (state) university buildings. The first demonstrations were held on 1 October in towns throughout Kosovo and involved people of all ages as well as students. They were broken up violently by police, leaving hundreds bruised or otherwise injured. Although further demonstrations at the end of October went ahead without police violence, hundreds more demonstrators were injured when police broke up the next demonstrations at the end of December.

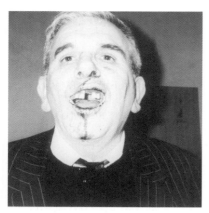

Sadri Fetiu, director of the Institute of Albanian studies in Priština

Police beat academics

On 8 March 1994, the authorities closed by force the Institute of Albanian studies in Pri‰otina, after orders to evacuate it were ignored by ethnic Albanians working at the Institute. On this occasion, groups of Serbian civilians (possibly plainclothes police), and armed police entered the building and beat those who had remained inside. In a statement published on 14 March, the CDHRF said that among those beaten and injured were the following academics: 'The director, Sadri Fetiu (who received injuries to his head, face, nose, jaw and had three teeth broken); Ragip Mulaku (injuries to his head, face, a rib and a fractured left hand); Professor Anton Çetta (injuries to his head, left hand and spine); Mehmet Halimi (injuries to a leg, a rib, and his head and face); the archivist Hajdin Hajdini (injuries to the face, head and both legs); Xheladin Shala (injuries to his body and head).'

Border-guard attacks

Ethnic Albanians have frequently complained of harassment at border crossings, generally when entering Yugoslavia from Hungary or at the border between Kosovo province and the Former Yugoslav Republic of Macedonia (FYROM). There have been numerous reports that border-guards have confiscated foreign currency or passports from travellers; there have also been complaints of physical ill-treatment.

M (his name is withheld at his request) is an ethnic Albanian living in France. In January 1994 he learned from his family that his father was gravely ill, and he therefore returned to Kosovo via Skopje in the Former Yugoslav Republic of Macedonia.

A week later, on his departure for France, he was detained by a border guard at Djeneral Janković on the Macedonian border, after the border guard noticed that M's passport contained a stamp showing he had visited Albania. (According to M, he went to Albania in 1992 in order to try to obtain a visa for France after being refused one in Belgrade.)

'... the officer who took my passport started insulting me together

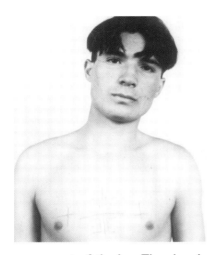

Student beaten

'Two police officers entered the bus and began to check the identity cards of the passengers. I was at the back of the bus. I saw them take out two young men through the front door. When they reached me, they asked me for my identity card. I gave it to them, and then one of the officers suddenly grabbed me by the hair and pulled me out of the bus. They handcuffed me and put me in their car. They took all three of us to the police station. They led us inside and separated us. They took me into a room and then the beating and torture began. Next they tied me to a radiator and three police officers sat on me; one of them pulled out a knife and after he had pulled up my shirt he cut a cross [on my chest] with the Cyrillic 'S'. After two hours they put me in a car and brought me back to the bus stop in Peć...'

The cross and four Cyrillic Ss stand for the Serbian motto: 'Only Unity Saves the Serb'.
Arian Curri, aged 18, was a secondary school student from the village of Gornji Streoci near Peć. He was on his way home from school by bus on 6 April 1994, when, on the outskirts of Peć, police boarded the bus and arrested him.

with another officer. They said I was one of those Albanian swine and an enemy of "Greater Serbia". They accused me of having been in Albania to buy weapons. Then they handcuffed me and placed me in a very small and dirty cell with a mud floor and nothing to lie down or even sit on. I stayed there about four hours until a plainclothes police inspector came to interrogate me. He... interrogated me for about an hour or so, asking about the reasons for my trip to Albania. [After] the inspector left, the two border guards started to ill-treat me. One in particular... was very brutal; he... punched me in the face and kicked my legs and back; he also hit me with a truncheon.' Two weeks later

Serb mother Maria Spašić weeps while waiting for news of her son Žarko, abducted in
May 1998, apparently by the Kosovo Liberation Army

traces of bruising were still visible on M's back and left arm.

'He spat in my face and insulted me... I was locked up again, handcuffed, in the cell. After a while he... came in with a hose and told me that dogs like me should be cleaned because they stank. He hosed me with very cold water... I was then left alone, wet and freezing, till the next morning. I was given nothing to eat or drink until midday, when I was at last given a cup of cold coffee. [The same officer] came back in the afternoon and started again to threaten me that he was ready to kill all Albanians, including me. He beat me again, slapping my face and hitting me with a truncheon. Finally, I don't know when exactly, I was 'granted' a second cold water shower with a fire hose. I was unable to sleep all night because I was freezing and I was afraid of dying of cold so I tried to move about as much as I could in that very small cell.'

According to M, the officer also confiscated M's money, wedding ring and some jewels his parents had given him to take to his wife in France as a wedding present. The following day M was driven to his home town in Kosovo where he was detained in police custody and interrogated for a further four days, before finally being released. He left the country soon after.

Abuses by opposition groups

The vast majority of the victims in Kosovo province have been ethnic Albanians. Nevertheless it must not be forgotten that in the current crisis Serbs are also suffering human rights abuses at the hands of armed ethnic Albanians.

The KLA has been held responsible for a number of abductions. The dead bodies of some of those abducted have been found left lying by roadsides. Amnesty International fears that others may remain undiscovered or buried in hidden graves.

The missing include both police and civilians, ethnic Serbs and Montenegrins, ethnic Albanians, and Roma. Some relatives of missing ethnic Albanians reported detained by the KLA believe that they may have been accused of 'collaborating' with the Serbian authorities, but claim that this was a trumped-up charge, possibly the result of a denunciation by someone settling a personal score.

Jakup Krasniqi, who has been named an official spokesman for the KLA, in an interview carried by the ARTA news agency on 12 July, stated: 'There are no kidnappings from our side. Even [if] there were some, the ones that were afflicted were the Albanian collaborationists more than the Serb civilians... We don't deal with civilians, the prisoners of war that we find we give them back... The ones that were kidnapped or we have kidnapped, we either give the list with their names, or we announce if someone gets executed...'

Although it is the case that some of those abducted have been returned – either informally released or handed over in procedures facilitated by the ICRC – many remain unaccounted for. Common Article 3 of the Geneva Conventions of 1949, which are binding on all participants in armed conflict, prohibits the killing of those taking no part in armed conflict, and prohibits hostage-taking. In the interview quoted above, Jakup Krasniqi stated that the KLA was aware of these provisions and intended to comply with them, but there is no available evidence that the KLA is taking serious steps to do so. On the contrary, Jakup Krasniqi's reference to executions in his statement underlines that the KLA is failing to respect Common Article 3 to the extent that it acknowledges executing some of the abducted. Therefore, Amnesty International is stressing the need for the KLA to reform and strengthen its chain of command, to ensure that such abuses in violation of Common Article 3 are not carried out, and to suspend from active duty pending investigation and appropriate disciplinary proceedings anyone suspected of committing such abuses.

There are persistent rumours that some of those abducted are alive, held in improvised camps and employed in manual labour such as digging trenches and fortifications for their captors, but it has not been possible to confirm these. One village frequently mentioned as the site of a detention camp is Likovac (Likovc) in the Dećane area, which was effectively under the control of the KLA from early in 1998. However, although Serbian forces briefly regained control of the village during the first week of August, there have been no reports that any detainees were found in the area.

Up to June 1998 the most detailed accounts of abuses by the armed opposition came from Glodjane village, in information compiled by the Humanitarian Law Centre (HLC). Following the March killing by police of three men in Glodjane, the KLA set up checkpoints at the entrances to the village. Three Serbian men, Dragoslav and Mijat Stojanovic and Veselin Stijovic, from the Dubrava hamlet, returned to their house on 18 April to collect some of their possessions. The Serbs were detained by uniformed men at their house where they were knocked to the ground and beaten. They were then taken to what they called the KLA headquarters in Glodjane, where they were further beaten with rifle butts and clubs during an interrogation. They were released the next day. One of them was reportedly treated in hospital for serious injuries to the spleen, stomach and duodenum. The victims stated that they recognised most of the perpetrators as local people whom they knew.

KLA beatings and executions

On 12 April 1998 two Serb men, Novak Stijovic and Staniša Radoševic, and the mother of the latter, Rosa Radoševic, went to the village of Pozar near Glodjane to collect the elderly father of Novak Stijovic. They were detained, beaten and questioned by armed ethnic Albanian men, who took them to the so-called KLA headquarters in Glodjane. They were made to retrieve and hand over a hunting rifle from one of their houses, before being released and allowed to leave in the direction of Dećane. Meanwhile, Staniša's father, Slobodan Radoševic, had stayed behind to look after their farm in Dašinovac village and his family has not had any news from him since. However, on 27 April the Kosovo Albanian language daily Koha Ditore reported that the KLA had executed five abducted Serbs, but did not give their names. According to the pro-government Media Centre in Priština the bodies of Slobodan Radoševic and that of another missing Serb, Miloš Radunovic, had been seen at the side of the road in Dašinovac. Neither of these reports has been independently confirmed.

Among Serbs and Montenegrins believed to have been abducted or held by members of the KLA are several women. On 21 April the majority of the Serb inhabitants of the village of Gornji Ratiš in the Dećane area fled when the KLA established control over the area. Among those who remained were the sisters Dara Vujošević (69) and Vukosava Vujošević (65), Milka Vlahović (62) and her husband Milovan (60). According to the daughter of Milka and Milovan Vlahovic, when she and her brother attempted to return on the following day in order to help their relatives leave, they were prevented from entering the village by members of the KLA. The fate of the four elderly people remains unknown.

Amnesty International is also concerned about the fate of the Šmigić family from the village of Leočina in the Drenica region. By 18 May most of the Serb inhabitants had abandoned the village, but a few remained behind; among them were Krstiva Šmigić and her relatives, Sultana Šmigić (72) and her husband Milosav (75), and Aleksandra (Lenka) Šmigić (c.75) and her son Radomir (54). Krstiva Šmigić later informed HLC researchers that, upon seeing armed KLA men enter the village, she ran over to Milosav and Sultana's house. When these men asked them: 'What are you doing here? This is Albania, there's nothing for you here', Milosav replied 'Till now this was Serbia but even if it's Albania, we'll talk it over and live together on good terms'. After he said this the men beat him with their rifle butts and kicked Krstiva and Sultana. They then ransacked the house, set fire to the beds and bedding and said they would come back in one hour. The elderly people decided to flee. Radomir and Lenka Šmigić, who had seen from their courtyard what was going on, called them over. They left Milosav in the courtyard and went over to Radomir and Lenka's house to decide where they would hide. Radomir told the women to go out and hide in the corn field and he would hide upstairs in the house. The women went outside but two of them decided to return to the house. In the meantime, some 30 armed men, some of whom were in KLA uniforms, had appeared in the courtyard. Ten of them entered and found Radomir upstairs. Immediately afterwards, Lenka and Krstiva heard screaming and Lenka ran inside the house and up the stairs. Krstiva stayed in the courtyard and heard: '...wailing and screaming, I couldn't bear to listen to it, even God wouldn't have been able to listen to such screams. Then I heard three gunshots and I went into the field'.

Krstiva then saw that the Šmigić houses were burning. When she walked over to Milosav's house the next day, calling to Sultana, Radomir and Lenka, nobody answered her. She spent the second and third night near the house and on the fourth night went to Rudnik where she knew there were police and Serbs.

Amnesty International is concerned that Milosav, Sultana, Radomir and Lenka Šmigić have gone 'missing' and may have been arbitrarily and summarily executed by members of the KLA.

On 19 May Dostana Šmigić (42), the daughter of Krstiva Šmigić, set off from her home in Srbica, in order to fetch her mother. A witness reportedly saw her car being stopped by a group of armed Albanians. Her whereabouts remain unknown, and although her family has received information that she is being held in the village of Likovac, it has not proved possible to confirm this.

6

Impunity: the final insult

Rrustem Sefedini, aged 48, was director of a secondary technical school in Uroševac until January 1991. He was then dismissed from his post because he did not implement the curriculum laid down by the Serbian authorities. In August the school was closed to ethnic Albanian pupils and ethnic Albanian staff were dismissed.

On 1 October Rrustem Sefedini organised a protest meeting against these measures. Three days later he was arrested by police after a further meeting. They questioned him and beat him so severely that they cracked three of his ribs. The following day he was sentenced to 60 days' imprisonment for disturbing 'public law and order', and was immediately sent to serve this sentence, despite being in great pain from his injuries.

At his trial Rrustem Sefedini complained to the judge that the police had beaten him; the judge refused to record his complaint in the minutes of the trial.

Human rights abuses by police are well-documented by human rights activists in Kosovo province and Serbia, by international human rights organisations and media, and have been condemned by the international community. Nonetheless, the authorities have failed to take measures to bring them to an end.

On the contrary, the authorities' response to condemnation of these abuses has been either to denounce this as part of an international campaign to promote Albanian secessionism, or more specifically, to deny abuses or imply that they are to be condoned when committed against those who break the law and seek secession. Yet both national law and the international human rights treaties which are legally binding on Yugoslavia explicitly prohibit torture and ill-treatment. Article 191 of the Yugoslav Criminal Code punishes, with up to three years' imprisonment, officials who in the performance of their duties physically ill-treat, intimidate or insult another person. Article 65 of the Serbian Criminal Code provides for a sentence of up to five years' imprisonment if the ill-treatment is intended to extract a confession (or up to 15 years if the ill-treatment is very serious). Torture or cruel, inhuman or degrading treatment or punishment are also prohibited under Article 7 of the International Covenant on Civil and Political Rights and under the UN Convention against Torture and Other Cruel, Inhuman or Degrading Treatment or Punishment, both treaties which are legally binding on the Federal Republic of Yugoslavia.

Responsibility for the police and judicial system is primarily in the hands of the Serbian republican authorities. The Yugoslav Army, which is now deployed in Kosovo, falls under the control of the Federal Authorities and the Yugoslav President, Slobodan Milošević, formerly President of Serbia. For years Amnesty International has repeatedly appealed to the authorities to fulfil their international legal obligations by carrying out investigations into many individual cases of alleged torture, ill-treatment or unlawful killing by police and to bring to justice those responsible. In practice, prosecutions of police officers (or soldiers) by the authorities are rare. In a few cases relatives of victims have initiated criminal proceedings. However, even before the 1998 conflict, ethnic Albanians were generally reluctant to use the Yugoslav legal system, for a variety of reasons, including a lack of confidence that anything would be achieved, and the sheer expense of a private prosecution. Such judicial proceedings frequently took years to complete.

Authorities deny beating

Amnesty International has repeatedly called on the Serbian authorities to investigate individual cases of alleged torture or other ill-treatment and to bring those responsible to justice. One such case was that of Sami Kurteshi, a member of an ethnic Albanian human rights organisation, the Council for the Defence of Human Rights and Freedom (CDHRF). On 7 July 1993, in the presence of colleagues, Kurteshi was beaten on the Council's premises in Priština by police carrying out a search and again afterwards in a local police station. He was released the same day. Amnesty International possesses a report of this incident issued by the Council the same day, a detailed statement by Sami Kurteshi dated 12 July, as well as a copy of a medical certificate issued on 8 July which records multiple bruising consistent with his account of his beating.

The authorities did not respond to Amnesty International's appeals until November 1993 when the Federal Ministry of Foreign Affairs issued a statement accusing Amnesty International of making 'uncorroborated and unverified allegations and accusations' and illustrated this with the case of Sami Kurteshi. According to the Ministry's statement, after checking 'with the republican and provincial authorities, it was established that a person with such a name was never detained or arrested...' The statement ignored the allegations of ill-treatment.

Toleration of police violence

The attitude to police abuses of the highest judicial official in Kosovo province is noted in a report submitted in February 1994 to the United Nations High Commission on Human Rights by Tadeusz Mazowiecki, Special Rapporteur of the HCHR. 'The Special Rapporteur has received, with grave concern, information from a reliable non-governmental organisation about a meeting with the President of the Priština Regional [District] Court in which the ill-treatment of detainees by the police was discussed. It was reported that the President of the Court supported such treatment when "crimes against the State" were involved, "irrespective of whether there was a conviction or not".'

Other judicial officials appear to share this view, or at least to show little enthusiasm for addressing the problem of police violence. In a letter, dated 24 August 1993, to a defence lawyer who had complained about the ill-treatment of his client, the Deputy President of the District Court of Priština wrote: 'As regards the conduct of police officers, this court is not able to influence their work'.

In this climate of official toleration of police violence, it was not surprising that the human rights situation in Kosovo deteriorated further. There has been a marked increase in official hostility towards international human rights monitoring in the province. In July 1993 the Organisation for Security and Cooperation in Europe (OSCE) was forced by the government of the Federal Republic of Yugoslavia to close down its mission of long duration in Kosovo. The UN Special Rapporteur on the former Yugoslavia was also refused permission to base staff long-term in the Federal Republic. Since then there has been no permanent monitoring mission in Kosovo.

A short-term OSCE mission did undertake a visit to Yugoslavia in 1998, but the Belgrade authorities emphasised that the prospect of reintroducing a permanent and expanded OSCE presence in Yugoslavia, including Kosovo province, is dependent on the country's reinstatement into the OSCE, from which it was expelled in 1992.

Nightmare in Donji Prekaz

On 5 and 6 March 1998 special police forces carried out another operation around the village of Donji Prekaz, some 10 kilometres from Likošane. At least 56 ethnic Albanians were killed in this operation. The main target was the home of Adem Jashari. He had been convicted in absentia of 'terrorism' in an unfair trial in a court in Priština in July 1997 and was sentenced to 20 years' imprisonment. In public statements by the police since the trial he had been referred to as being a KLA commander. At the trial itself he was alleged to have received military training in Albania, to have recruited men to fight with the KLA and to have ordered and taken part in armed attacks against the police. Adem Jashari had allowed himself to be photographed with weapons by journalists who visited his family home in previous months. It appears that the police had been aware of his whereabouts for some time: in January the police launched an operation against his home village of Donji Prekaz but withdrew after an armed battle. From at least this time the police maintained a presence in a disused munitions factory in the vicinity of the village.

Although the full information about what happened in Donji Prekaz on 5 and 6 March is still not available, it seems that at least some of those killed were extrajudicially executed. Others may have been unlawfully killed as a result of the excessive force used without regard to the fact that women, children and unarmed men were among those in the houses when they were attacked by the police. There appears not to have been any intention either to effect the arrest of armed suspects in the village with proper precautions, or to minimise the use of force in order to protect life, as both national and international law requires. Rather, the operation appears to have been carried out as a military operation by forces under apparent orders to eliminate the suspects and their families.

The police operation was carried out or at least led by officers of the Special Police Units. These are elite units which are trained for special operations, such as dealing with hijacking. It is impossible to ascertain how many police officers were involved, but it seems likely that there were several hundred men. They were dressed in combat uniform, operated in military formations, and were supported by armoured personnel carriers (APCs) armed with heavy machine guns and cannons of at least 20 millimetre calibre. Besides vehicle-mounted weapons it appears that the police also carried heavy machine guns, rocket-propelled grenade launchers, assault rifles and sniper rifles. Some reports indicate that 81 millimetre mortar rounds were also fired in the attack.

In a report by the Serbian Ministry of Internal Affairs made public on 10 March the Ministry claimed that Adem Jashari had been involved in the attack on the police patrol near Likošane on 28

February.[11] The report also stated that there was another attack on a police patrol near Donji Prekaz on Thursday 5 March at dawn (at around 5.30am that day).

However, witnesses interviewed by Amnesty International and others give accounts that give strong reason to question this version of events. In particular, witnesses from other parts of the village than the Jasharis report the police moving in on and shooting at their homes from as early as 5.30 am. Witnesses from the Jasharis' part of the village described how their part was fired upon from about 6.30 am.

It is more difficult to estimate the degree of resistance offered by the armed ethnic Albanians in the Jashari compound and other parts of the village, particularly as some witnesses may have been reluctant to reveal knowledge of this. On the basis of what can be ascertained or deduced, it appears that each family or group of families gathered women, children and men who were not carrying arms into the safest room in each house. Meanwhile, some or all of the male members of each family repelled the police attack with arms. It also appears that they were expecting the police to attack, as they had done in the police action against the Jashari house in January, and in the incidents around Likošane a few days before. Nevertheless, it is evident that they were outnumbered, and had fewer and inferior weapons than the police used. They may well have had dozens of men armed with assault rifles and some other weapons such as anti-tank weapons. The degree of resistance offered from each house or group of houses also seems to have varied, but it is clear that the strongest resistance came from the Jashari compounds.

The only reported survivor from the compound where Adem Jashari's closest family members lived was an 11-year-old girl, BJ, who spoke to foreign and local journalists.[12] She told reporters how her family sheltered together during hours of firing in which her house was repeatedly hit and then, when the firing ceased, how she found the dead bodies of her three sisters Blerina (age seven years), Fatima (eight) and Lirie (10) and then of her mother and four brothers. Because of the lack of other witnesses and the concealment or destruction of evidence which will be described later, it is extremely difficult to reconstruct what happened in the compound except for

[11] Reported in *Tanjug* (Yugoslav news agency), relayed by BBC Monitoring Service, 11 March 1998.
[12] *Kosovo's silent houses of the dead*, Sunday Times (London) by Marie Colvin, 15 March 1998.

what the girl told journalists after her escape.

Around 35 children, women and some men gathered in a house across the track from Shaban Jashari's compound during the attack. Amnesty International interviewed most of the family groups which had been sheltering in the house. In their testimony, which was taken at separate locations, they largely corroborated each other, confirming details of the attack as a whole and describing in various degrees of detail the extrajudicial execution of three of the six men who had been with them and the wounding of a fourth.

The witnesses stated that after hearing the start of the attack at around 6.30am or 7am they gathered in the house of Beqir Jashari which had the strongest walls and was in the middle of the row of houses. They remained in the house listening to the sounds of the attack on the other houses until about 1.30 that afternoon. At this point they stated that the second and then first floors of Beqir Jashari's house came under fire and that the roof and upper part of the house started to collapse. Police then came close to the house and witnesses describe how a tear-gas grenade (this could possibly have been a smoke grenade) was thrown and the gas or smoke came into the room through the broken windows. Police then ordered the people to come out of the house one by one, calling in a mixture of Albanian and Serbian. In the confusion (the children did not understand the orders) the people in the house came out in groups with the men among them, some dressed in women's clothes. The men were picked out after they came out.

Mother witnesses son's killing

Twenty-six-year-old Nazmi Jashari was walking with his 70-year-old mother. Her account of his killing, parts of which follow, was corroborated by several other witnesses who were interviewed independently by Amnesty International.

'When we arrived at the door of the yard he said to me "Let me help you". ...When we went out of the yard my son held me. He told me "Okay mother, let's go", the only thing which I know from him. In front of the house when we were stopped they [the police] took my son from me. ... I told him go and leave me here because nothing will happen to me. He didn't say anything to me and they took my son from me until I turned my eyes to him .... they ordered my son to lie down, then they searched him and ordered him to get up again and he did that. Again to lie down, they did not find anything, no weapons. I saw with my eyes how they prepared their automatic weapons, two of them, one on one side and another on the other, they shot him between the shoulders. I saw that with my eyes and screamed at that moment "Please God, I rely on you!" ... I didn't know what else I could say. I held those two walking sticks. I felt that my feet were completely cold. I could not feel them, I didn't know that they were mine. I saw how he was still, he didn't move, he seemed to be sleeping. I thought to go and to see him, but one of the police ordered me: "Don't move!" He did not let me and I just stayed and looked. Then I wanted again to go and to cover him. I wanted to take this [her scarf] off and one of them turned a gun on me. He didn't let me.'

Whether or not all or some of the men who had been in the Beqir Jashari house were bearing arms during the police attack, it is important to stress that in the witnesses' accounts they had ceased to offer resistance and had effectively surrendered themselves to the police.

As the witnesses fled they described meeting or seeing several cordons of police after leaving their houses. They were directed to flee in the direction of a neighbouring village and most complained that police appeared to fire at the ground in their direction as they fled. There appeared to be no attempt by the police to organise a place of safety for them or to provide any medical or other assistance.

Witnesses from other places in the Jasharis' part of the village described variously how they were ordered out of their homes or how their homes were fired upon. Some hid in their own or neighbours' houses for two or three days. The houses in the Jasharis' part of the village were rendered uninhabitable; houses appeared to have been deliberately set on fire and parts were bulldozed with tracked vehicles during the operation.

In the aftermath of the incident, around 56 people were buried, amid some confusion. For example, at least two of the bodies handed over by the police came from Lauša village and had been killed in another incident. Some of the bodies were not identified because they had been badly burnt. Of around 41 bodies which were identified, 12 were women and 11 were children up to 16 years of age. Some of the survivors believe that bodies still remain in the ruined houses.

In the absence of more detailed evidence, the conclusion must be that the victims who were clearly not using arms – that is, the women and children at least – died as a result of the excessive use of force by the police in contravention of international standards on law enforcement. Little regard appears to have been taken of the fact that unarmed people were present in the houses. The women and child victims appeared to have died as a result of different combinations of shrapnel injuries, bullet wounds and falling debris inside the houses. International standards such as the UN Body of Principles on the Use of Force and Firearms by Law Enforcement Officials specify that intentional lethal use of firearms may only be made when strictly unavoidable in order to protect life. In particular no warning was given of the intention to use force before at least two houses were attacked with heavy machine guns, cannons and probably mortar rounds. According to witnesses, the police only called them to come out after several hours of bombardment.

Despite the reports from the Ministry of the Interior which implied that the police operation had been staged as an immediate response to an attack on a police patrol, the operation had the appearance of one which had been planned sometime in advance. This would have been all the more likely since the police had attacked the Adem Jashari compound in January and were fought off. Despite the evident opportunity to plan this operation there appears to be no pretence that the operation was aimed at simply arresting those suspected of alleged terrorist acts.

Evidence destroyed, dignity denied

The Federal Code of Criminal Procedure (CCP) specifies in Article 252 that autopsies shall be carried out when it is suspected that a death was caused by a criminal act or in connection with the carrying out of a criminal act. When an investigating magistrate is unable to attend the scene immediately, the police are allowed to initiate forensic investigations, but not to order autopsies (Article 154). However, in the aftermath of the operation the CCP appears to have been blatantly ignored. One witness who remained hidden in the village until 8 March stated that he saw the police removing the bodies without any particular care. At the same time they destroyed everything they laid their hands on.

According to the Council for the Defence of Human Rights and Freedoms, on 9 March the police in Srbica telephoned the CDHRF's sub-council in Srbica and told them that the bodies of those killed in Donji Prekaz were available for the CDHRF or others to come and arrange identification and burial. On 10 March the bodies were laid out in an undignified manner by the authorities in an open-sided building close to a road on the outskirts of Srbica. The bodies were apparently unprotected from interference by animals or other possible damage.

Many relatives complained that they were unable to pass police checkpoints to get to the bodies or the mass funeral which was held the next day. A delegation of ethnic Albanian doctors from Priština which was told by police that they would be able to view the bodies on 10 March was reportedly turned back twice by police despite assurances given by telephone that they would be able to pass police checkpoints. They did not reach the bodies. A convoy of the International Committee of the Red Cross (ICRC) and International Federation of Red Cross and Red Crescent Societies (IFRC) with delegates and medical supplies was also refused passage to the depot and the Drenica area. A truckload of coffins with the convoy was taken by the police and used for the burial.

Those representatives of the ethnic Albanian community who were able to reach the site where the bodies were laid out tried to organise an informal identification by those relatives who were able to reach the site. The police had apparently carried out their own identification of some of the bodies: they had numbered them and marked some as 'unidentified'. Photographs taken at the depot show no signs that autopsies had been carried out on the bodies.

On the following day, 11 March, relatives and others organising the funerals found that police had buried the bodies, carrying out threats which they had previously made that they would do so if the ethnic Albanians did not bury them quickly. The ethnic Albanian representatives then disinterred the coffins, tried to identify as many bodies as possible and reburied the bodies with the heads pointing towards Mecca in accordance with Muslim custom.

Amnesty International is seriously concerned at the failure of the authorities to carry out proper investigations into the causes of the deaths, in breach of national law as well as international standards relating to the investigation of killings in the course of police operations. The most glaring evidence of this is the lack of autopsies. The authorities claim that investigating magistrates were summoned to the scene; if this was the case then the failure to ensure autopsies were carried out appears to have been a gross dereliction of duty. The relatives of the dead suffered, and indeed continue to suffer, from the lack of proper information about how the victims died and the lack of any proper effort to ascertain responsibility. Moreover, only 40 or so of the 56 bodies were identified, leaving the grieving relatives of those missing who were not identified among victims in an even worse state. That the authorities appear to have actively blocked or prevented efforts to identify the bodies confirms the suspicion that many of the killings may have been extrajudicial executions.

Two ethnic Albanians unload flour in a village in Drenica region, where thousands were displaced by Yugoslav army and Serb police offensives (August 1998)

7

Refugees: victims of mass expulsion

'The situation in Kosovo is deteriorating... I must emphasise that while UNHCR and its partners stand ready to continue to help the victims, firm political action is urgently needed to resolve the crisis.'

Sadako Ogata, United Nations High Commissioner for Refugees, July 1998

Tens of thousands of people have been forced by the conflict in Kosovo province to flee their homes. The risks involved in flight are huge. At the mercy of dangerous border crossings, difficult terrain and continued fighting, displaced families head for wherever they think they have a chance of being safe.

Families have become separated. Ten-year-old Antigona Tishukaj, who became separated from her parents in the chaos that surrounded the destruction of her village in Kosovo in June 1998, walked for four days across the mountains between Kosovo and Albania. She eventually was reunited with her mother and cousin across the border.

Reports about the displaced from Kosovo province inevitably often state that 'many were women and children'. Each of the tens of thousands of victims has his or her own personal tragedy. They have seen their loved ones killed, their villages destroyed, their livelihoods ruined. Many of those who leave their homes wait within sight of their houses for hours, even days, before the spectacle of destruction and looting finally forces them to give up any hope of going back.

For those who take flight, the suffering is rarely over. Many have had to cross territory where battles are still raging. They are in urgent need of food and shelter. Already in danger because of their position, they are even more vulnerable because of who they are – the majority being women, children and the elderly. The internally displaced within

Kosovo, and those who have crossed into Albania, continue to be at risk in some places where they have sought refuge due to the highly volatile security situation. Even humanitarian organisations have been forced to withdraw from some parts of the area due to the extremely dangerous conditions.

According to interviews with refugees undertaken by representatives of the United Nations High Commissioner for Refugees, the usual sequence of events is that villages are shelled by Yugoslav forces from a distance, and most of the population then leaves. New arrivals in Albania say that there are still many in the Dećane-Djakovica area who want to cross the border into Albania. Others move from village to village, or stay in remote mountain areas far from their homes, in search of a safe place. Most have next to no possessions, not even ID cards or passports. Once in Albania, many live very near to the border with Kosovo province, especially in Tropoje commune. Tropoje is an arms-trafficking area and a place of military strategic importance: the security situation is highly volatile.

There are also acute economic problems. For example, Kosovar refugees in Albania have found themselves in a district which is probably the poorest in the European continent, with 50 per cent unemployment and barely able to support its own population. These economic problems have been aggravated by having to deal with the large number of refugees; there is a dire need for international support to alleviate the situation.

Still inside Kosovo, there have been reports of people hiding in their homes and basements, either stranded with no place to flee to or remaining in the hope that they will be safe if they stay where they are. Elsewhere, villages are deserted, and families have been found taking refuge in woods – with only trees as their shelter – afraid to go back to their village. In the town of Orahovac, where fighting raged in the second half of July 1998, thousands of people, mainly women and children, were found still hiding in their homes and basements, many of them without water and electricity.

In August 1998 it was estimated that there are some 170,000 people internally displaced within the borders of the Federal Republic of Yugoslavia. This is in addition to those refugees who have fled to other countries such as Albania during the course of 1998. In the Tropoje district of Norther Albania there were estimated to be over 6,000 such refugees

Fighting around Peć and Dećane in particular caused many to make the mountainous crossing into Montenegro, a journey beset with dangers. For those who move to neighbouring villages or areas within Kosovo, the earlier pattern of hospitality, with relatives and friends opening their houses to a large number of families, has begun to erode. In some areas the internally displaced population is some 30 per cent of the total local population. One aid worker reported: 'Hungry children are standing in the streets in their underwear looking for food. Residents took in refugees for free at first, but with the numbers increasing they are starting to charge money. The situation is terrible.'

The strain of this influx on local populations means that there is no other choice but for the displaced to go to collective centres – some lacking necessary sanitary facilities and other basics such as electricity and water. The challenges presented to those surviving in these conditions are enormous: for example, the vast influx into Montenegro has meant that many people were crammed into ramshackle buildings without power, water, regular food or medical care. Where the humanitarian assistance agencies trying to provide shelter and care are not able to operate safely in the area, the situation is even more desperate.

Refugees who bear for years the scars from the dislocation, traumatisation and violation of their fundamental human rights are the legacy of conflicts in many parts of the world. History has, time and again, shown that the story of refugees fleeing conflict is largely the story of women and children. They are particularly vulnerable before, during and after their flight from their country of origin. Women in flight may be attacked by bandits, smugglers, or other refugees. When they arrive at borders they are vulnerable to border guards or security forces forcing them back or attempting to extort money or sexual favours for allowing safe passage. In particular, women who have been separated from male family members are vulnerable to abuse and exploitation and, in numerous refugee movements that the world has witnessed, women refugees have been subject to rape and sexual assault. These are but a few of the dangers refugees face when conflict rages and they are forced to flee in search of safety.

The continued fighting between KLA and Serbian forces has rendered organized return of the internally displaced to their homes out of the question, and as fighting has spread, it has also put them at increased risk. In June UNHCR representatives visited a camp of some 600 ethnic Albanians in the mountainous area between Junik village and the Albanian border. 'The overcrowded shelters and harsh mountainous environment made for extremely unsanitary conditions,'

Kosovar refugees arrive on Albanian soil after a mountain crossing (June 1998)

they later reported. 'Families [are] living in tents and make-shift shelters made from branches, logs and plastic sheeting. People had few clothes and shoes. In addition, a presence of snakes, rodents and insects put the group at risk.' Those interviewed also said their food supplies were dwindling, and they lacked access to basic medical care.

Xhemile Tahiraj (35) from the village of Ereć is one of the many women who has been internally displaced. During the second week of April she and her husband Hasan Tahiraj became concerned for her safety and that of their five year old daughter Eldiana. She left the village to stay with relatives in the nearby town of Djakovica. On 25 April Xhemile Tahiraj heard that her husband was one of a group of men from Ereć killed on 23 April in a clash on the border with Army forces while attempting to obtain arms and bring them into Kosovo. She decided to return to the village to say a last farewell to her husband, travelling by village paths as she feared using the main road would be unsafe.

Albanian sources have claimed that there was some shelling of the village that day. Xhemile Tahiraj said that she decided to return to her house, as she heard gunshots and the sound of shelling. She said: 'I opened the gate into the courtyard, and was about to enter when I felt that I was wounded and my legs gave way beneath me. I noticed blood on my hand. My daughter Eli was also bloody. I barely managed to get inside and call for help before I collapsed unconscious.'

Xhemile Tahiraj was helped to a private doctor, and later transferred to hospital in Djakovica, where she required an operation to remove a bullet from her leg. Although her daughter had lost blood from her injury she did not require an operation.

Many women have said that they were forced to leave villages under indiscriminate attack by Serb forces. F.H. from the village of Popoci told Amnesty International delegates that she was in the courtyard of her house in the early morning in April, preparing to milk the cows, when she heard shooting and the sound of shelling. The family made their escape on a tractor, hiding in the woods and not daring to light a fire for fear that they would be seen and shot at. She believes that her house was burned, along with others in the village.

M.H. from Shatej in the Djakovica region described her village coming under heavy shelling and taking shelter in a cellar along with around 80 women, children and elderly people. Although the shelling continued she and her daughter and grandson headed for the village of Gramoçel where they sheltered for three nights. Although she reported

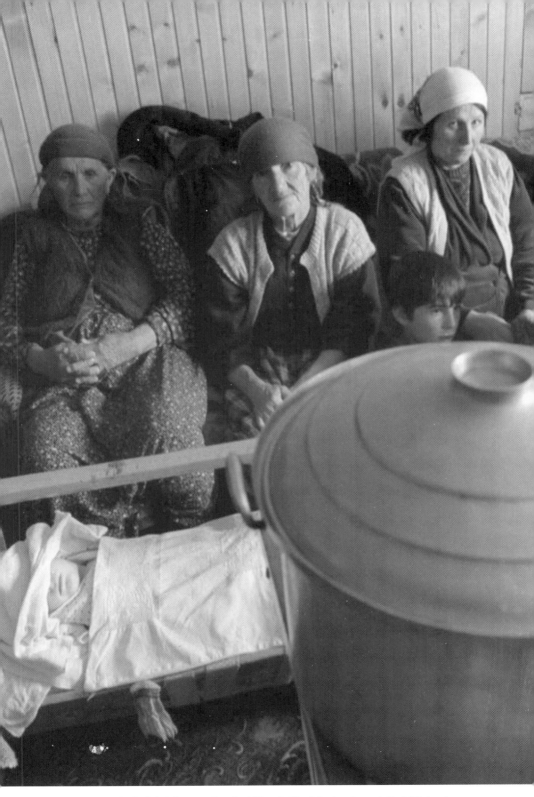

Ethnic Albanian women who fled their homes after the killings in Donji Prekaz, in a relative's kitchen in a neighbouring village (March 1998)

that the shelling was less heavy, she was wounded in the leg, and she finally made her way to Djakovica, although shooting continued.

In addition to those internally displaced in the Federal Republic of Yugoslavia, many people have fled their country to seek asylum, and many more could do so. In the light of the pattern of serious human rights violations in Kosovo, states are reminded of their obligations under international law to allow access to their territories to those fleeing in search of safety. States should respect the fundamental principle of non-refoulement and refrain from turning back at their borders those who seek asylum. The international community should meet its obligations to share responsibility for those in need of international protection.

Amnesty International is concerned that any action by the international community should not include measures which violate the fundamental human rights to leave one's country and to seek asylum. The international community should not pursue any policies that prevent those fleeing from obtaining effective protection across borders if necessary.

As well as those who are currently in flight, there are an estimated 150,000 rejected asylum-seekers from the Federal Republic of Yugoslavia, most of them Kosovo Albanians, in Western Europe. Amnesty International welcomes the announcements in 1998 by some states hosting rejected asylum-seekers from Kosovo to suspend returns. The organisation urges all states to suspend returns to Kosovo, until such time as there is no risk of returnees facing threats of serious human rights violations.

The plea in July 1998 of Sadako Ogata, United Nations High Commissioner for Refugees, for urgent political action to resolve the crisis in Kosovo is a grim reminder of her call to the international community for help during the crises in the Great Lakes region of Africa and elsewhere in the former Yugoslavia.

International community's failure

The armed confrontation in Kosovo province has provoked a worldwide outcry not to permit 'another Bosnia'. Yet some of the same governments denouncing alleged 'ethnic cleansing' in Kosovo are pursuing dangerous policies towards the repatriation of refugees from other parts of former Yugoslavia. This falls far short of a just remedy for serious human rights violations.

From governments around the world, strong words on Kosovo

sound hollow when we look at the current approach by the international community to 'resolving' the problem of mass expulsion in Bosnia-Herzegovina. Some governments seem more interested in ridding themselves of their perceived refugee 'burden' than in ending the agony that refugees face.

Current repatriation policies by certain governments threaten to make concrete the results of the mass expulsion in Bosnia-Herzegovina. Moreover, reported plans to send large numbers of Bosnian Croats to Croatia would quite certainly make permanent the forcible exile of Croatian Serbs who fled but want to return to their homes. Such repatriation policies in fact cement the previous conflicts' objectives – the creation of territories inhabited by a single nationality. What this says to the authorities behind the human rights violations is that if they are patient enough to sit out the international community's criticism, they will eventually realise their goals when the international community loses interest in promoting fair solutions.

In looking for protection for those fleeing human rights violations in the Kosovo crisis, the international community should learn from – and remedy – the policy failures over Bosnia-Herzegovina and Croatia.

Lessons from Croatia and Bosnia-Herzegovina

Croatian politicians reported in May 1998 that a joint German-Croatian parliamentarians' working group had discussed a Croatian government invitation to resettle 80,000 Bosnian Croat refugees. Then in Germany, they would be returned to Croatia later in the year. Amnesty International fears that Bosnian Croats sent to Croatia would be accommodated in housing owned by Croatian Serbs. It appears that the plan is intended by the Croatian authorities as a means to prevent the return of Croatian Serbs, by making sure that they have nowhere to go. Furthermore, an agreement by the Croatian authorities to accept such a large number of refugees is wholly inconsistent with the authorities' complaints that they cannot manage the return of large numbers of their own citizens – Croatian Serbs.

Human rights violations have prevented the return of Croatian Serb refugees and displaced people to their pre-war homes. In fact, people continue to flee from within the tiny remaining community of Croatian Serbs. The authorities in Croatia frequently respond to calls that they should facilitate the return of Croatian Serbs by pointing to the plight of Bosnian Croat refugees in Croatia. Many come from areas of Bosnia-Herzegovina where, if they were to return, they would now be in a minority, and for them too it is not safe to return.

The Humanitarian Issues Working Group (HIWG) declared 1998 to be the year of 'minority return', allowing the return of refugees and displaced people to pre-war communities where their nationality is now in the minority. This is a positive effort by the international community to remedy the violation of mass expulsion. Authorities should improve the human rights situation so that people, regardless of their nationality, can return to their own homes in safety if they so choose. Nevertheless, given the risks that face those who do choose to return, the increased efforts in 1998 should not be interpreted by host countries of asylum as a green light to send back minorities.

Contrary to the advice of the UNHCR, early in 1998 German *länder* forcibly repatriated refugees from Bosnia-Herzegovina who would now be minorities if they returned to their pre-war homes. The consequence for most such people is that they are forced to relocate to areas where their national group is a majority, which in turn creates an obstacle for the minorities who wish to return there. The pace of forcible repatriations has doubled: so far in 1998, Bavaria, Berlin, Brandenburg, Hesse, North Rhine-Westphalia, Saarland, Saxony, and Thuringia *länder* all have policies which allow for the forcible repatriation of Bosnian refugees who would now be in a minority if they returned to their pre-war homes.

8

From Nuremburg to the Balkans

'Crimes against international law are committed by men, not by abstract entities, and only by punishing individuals who commit such crimes can the provisions of international law be enforced.'

From the judgment of the International Military Tribunal at Nuremberg

It is the failure of the Federal Republic of Yugoslavia's government and the international community to hold to account those responsible for longstanding abuses that has led to today's human rights crisis.

Amnesty International takes no position on the political status of Kosovo. It is, however, deeply concerned about the large-scale human rights violations against ethnic Albanians either because of their direct involvement with political struggle or simply because of their nationality. The Federal Republic of Yugoslavia is a party to international human rights instruments such as the International Covenant on Civil and Political Rights (ICCPR). It is thus under obligations to protect the basic human rights of all of its citizens, irrespective of their nationality.

It is clear that the protection of human rights is one issue among others to be resolved in the crisis in Kosovo province. However, lack of respect for human rights in the past, coupled with the fact that those who committed human rights violations have rarely been brought to account, has been a major contributor to the political instability and current conflict. Moreover, the indications are that the situation will continue to deteriorate and that human rights violations could become still more grave.

International outrage – but no resolve

International deliberations of the Contact Group and others regarding Kosovo province over the summer of 1998 were primarily a response to the rapidly deteriorating security situation and the outbreak of open conflict. However, the international community's analysis and response should dig deeper than media headlines. The current situation cannot be isolated from a decade of unaddressed human rights violations in Kosovo province.

Given the endemic lack of accountability and the legacy of injustice in Kosovo, it is vital for any lasting solution to the present crisis to address explicitly and comprehensively the need for durable guarantees for human rights protection; the accountability of those responsible for past and present human rights violations by police and security forces; and effective reparation for all victims of human rights violations.

The international community has warned Yugoslav President Slobodan Milošević that it will not tolerate 'another Bosnia' (referring to the 1992 to 1995 armed conflict where civilians were the targets of appalling human rights violations during military actions because of their nationality). Nevertheless, one of the lessons so far learned from previous armed conflicts in the region is that the international community will not sustain its outrage. Nearly all those suspects known to be indicted by the International Criminal Tribunal for the former Yugoslavia who remain at large were part of Serbian military, paramilitary, policing or civilian authorities in Bosnia-Herzegovina and Croatia. If the international community wants to send a message to President Milošević that it is serious about holding human rights violators to account, it should do so by showing its resolve in other areas of the region.

War crimes

War crimes and crimes against humanity have been committed in 1998 in Kosovo province. Members of the Yugoslav army and the Serbian police have been responsible for enforced disappearances and the extrajudicial execution of civilian non-combatants. The Serbian police have engaged in the widespread torture of suspects, sometimes leading to their deaths. These acts constitute grave breaches of humanitarian law and international human rights law.

Members of the Kosovo Liberation Army have been responsible for the killings of people not involved in hostilities and for abductions and the taking of hostages. This is prohibited by Common Article 3 of the Geneva Conventions of 1949 and constitutes a serious breach of humanitarian law.

Individuals responsible for planning or carrying out such acts should be held to have personal criminal responsibility, in line with the principle established at the Nuremberg Tribunal after the Second World War. Ensuring that this is the case is one of the most important interventions the international community could make to halt future bloodshed in Kosovo province.

The International Criminal Tribunal for the former Yugoslavia was established by UN Security Council Resolution 827/1993 with the power to prosecute persons for genocide, crimes against humanity, grave breaches of the Geneva Conventions of 1949 and violations of the laws and customs of war committed in the territory of the former Socialist Federal Republic of Yugoslavia since 1 January 1991. The Tribunal's jurisdiction thus includes the geographical area of the Federal Republic of Yugoslavia, including Kosovo province. The Tribunal has concurrent jurisdiction with the national courts of the Federal Republic of Yugoslavia to prosecute violations.

The Tribunal must be properly funded and given all the necessary political support to carry out its mandate to investigate and prosecute grave breaches of international humanitarian law and crimes against humanity in Kosovo province. The Tribunal's investigators and forensic experts need access to all areas, including grave sites, in the province.

The international community can help ensure that the former Yugoslavia takes a decisive step to break with the past. They can send a strong message that they will not tolerate these crimes, and that the full weight of the law will be brought to bear on those responsible for them. They can help end the cycle of impunity which currently encourages human rights violations.

Recommendations

1. To the international community

• The international community should assist the International Criminal Tribunal for the former Yugoslavia in its efforts to investigate the situation in Kosovo province and to prosecute those responsible for war crimes and crimes against humanity. They should provide the Tribunal with all the necessary financial and other support required to carry out its mandate effectively.

• The international community should provide financial resources and political support to an enlarged human rights monitoring programme

On trial in the Hague: Bosnian Serb Mirosla Kvocka and Mladen Radic in the stand of the International Criminal Tribunal for the former Yugoslavia, watched by a UN security guard.

of the Office of the United Nations High Commissioner for Human Rights (OHCHR) in the Federal Republic of Yugoslavia, enabling its field operation to monitor effectively human rights in the country as a whole, including an adequately staffed field office in Kosovo.

• Given the fundamental human right to leave one's country and seek asylum, states should not pursue any policies that prevent those forced from their homes from obtaining effective protection against borders if necessary. States should respect the fundamental principle of *non-refoulement* of refugees, and share responsibility for those in need of international protection.

2. To the Yugoslavian and Serbian authorities

Of course, the prime responsibility to improve the human rights situation rests with the national authorities. Amnesty International calls on the Yugoslavian federal and Serbian national authorities to:

• Issue clear instructions to all police and other security personnel in Kosovo that deliberate and indiscriminate attacks on civilians, arbitrary arrests and expulsions and other human rights violations will not be tolerated under any circumstances and that those responsible will be held criminally responsible for their actions.

• Allow immediate and unhindered access to the area for humanitarian agencies and UN human rights monitors. The OHCHR should now be granted the facilities to establish a constant presence in Priština.

• Allow the International Committee of the Red Cross (ICRC) unrestricted access to all areas of Kosovo and permit the organisation to visit all prisoners it requests to see, in accordance with established procedures.

• Cooperate fully with the International Criminal Tribunal in any investigations it may wish to conduct in Kosovo and permit forensic experts to carry out their professional duties without restrictions.

• Disclose the identity and whereabouts of those detained and instruct the police and other armed forces to allow those detained prompt access to lawyers – measures vital for the prevention of torture and to safeguard against enforced disappearances.

• Order prompt and impartial investigations into reports of human rights violations, ensure that those responsible are held fully accountable and that victims or their families receive effective reparation.

3. To the armed political opposition in Kosovo province

Amnesty International is also deeply concerned by killings and other human rights abuses reportedly committed by armed opposition groups in Kosovo province, and recommends that:

• The Kosovo Liberation Army and any other armed opposition groups in Kosovo province must ensure that all forces under their control abide by basic humanitarian law principles as set out in Common Article 3 of the Geneva Conventions of 1949 which prohibits the killing, ill-treatment or hostage-taking of civilians and insists on the humane treatment of captured enemy forces.

• The KLA should ensure that it cooperates with the ICRC and other international humanitarian agencies to ascertain the whereabouts and fate of prisoners reportedly detained by its members.

Ethnic Albanian women hold up blank pieces of paper to symbolise their lack of rights in Kosovo (1998)

Bibliography

Amnesty International reports:

Document Series A: Events to June 1998
  #1: Background: A crisis waiting to happen (AI Index: EUR 70/32/98)
  #2: *Violence in Drenica* (AI Index: EUR 70/33/98)
  #3: *Deaths in custody, torture and ill-treatment* (AI Index: EUR 70/34/98)
  #4: *Unfair trials and abuses of due process* (AI Index: EUR 70/35/98)
  #5: *Ljubenic and Poklek: A pattern repeated* (AI Index: EUR 70/46/98)

Kosovo province: A decade of human rights violations Amnesty International UK, June 1998

Yugoslavia: Police violence against ethnic Albanians in Kosovo province AI Index: EUR 70/06/94, 1994

Yugoslavia: Police violence in Kosovo province - the victims AI Index: EUR 70/16/94, 1994

Yugoslavia: Ethnic Albanians - Trial by truncheon AI Index: EUR 70/01/94, 1994

FR Yugoslavia - International monitoring in Kosovo and beyond: Appeal to governments from Secretary General of Amnesty International AI Index: EUR 70/23/93, 1993

Yugoslavia: Ethnic Albanians - Victims of torture and ill-treatment by police in Kosovo province AI Index: EUR 48/18/92, 1992

Yugoslavia: Amnesty International's Current Concerns AI Index: EUR 48/01/91, 1991

Yugoslavia: Administrative Detention ('Isolation') Torture Allegations AI Index: EUR 48/13/89, 1989

Yugoslavia: Recent Events in the Autonomous Province of Kosovo AI Index: EUR 48/08/89, 1989

Yugoslavia: Ethnic Albanians on Trial in Kosovo Province AI Index: EUR 48/19/89, 1989

The Amnesty International Mandate

Amnesty International is a worldwide voluntary movement of 1.1 million people that works to prevent some of the gravest violations by governments of people's fundamental human rights. The main focus of its campaigning is to:

- free all prisoners of conscience. These are people detained anywhere for their beliefs, or by reason of their ethnic origin, sex, colour, language, national or social origin, economic status, birth, or other status – who have not used or advocated violence;
- ensure fair and prompt trials for political prisoners;
- abolish the death penalty, torture and other cruel treatment of prisoners;
- end extra-judicial executions and 'disappearances'.

Amnesty International, also opposes abuses by opposition groups: hostage-taking, torture and killings of prisoners and other arbitrary killings.

Amnesty International is impartial. It is independent of any government, political persuasion or religious creed. It does not support or oppose any government or political system, nor does it support or oppose views of the victims whose rights it seeks to protect. It is concerned solely with the protection of the human rights involved in each case, regardless of the ideology of the government, opposition forces or the beliefs of the individual. Amnesty International is financed by sub-scriptions and donations from its world-wide membership. No funds are sought or accepted from governments.

Amnesty International, recognising that human rights are indivisible and inter-dependent, works to promote all the human rights enshrined in the Universal Declaration of Human Rights and other international standards, through its human rights education programmes and campaigning for ratification of human rights treaties.

For more information and details of membership contact:

Amnesty International United Kingdom
99-119 Rosebery Avenue, London, EC1R 4RE
Tel: 0171-814 6200   Fax: 0171-833 1510
Website: http://www.amnesty.org.uk/

Ethnic Albanians cross the mountains to escape Serb attacks on their villages (June 1998)